*The Social Sources of
Denominationalism*

THE SOCIAL SOURCES OF DENOMINATIONALISM

by H. RICHARD NIEBUHR

LIVING AGE BOOKS

published by MERIDIAN BOOKS, INC. *New York*

H. Richard Niebuhr, one of the outstanding representatives of Protestant theology in the United States, teaches in the Divinity School of Yale University. He is the author, in addition to *The Social Sources of Denominationalism*, of *Christ and Culture* and *The Meaning of Revelation*.

Copyright © 1929 by Henry Holt and Company, Inc.

Reprinted by arrangement with The Shoe String Pre

Published by Meridian Books March 1957
First printing February 1957
Second printing April 1958

Library of Congress Catalog Card Number: 57-6685
Manufactured in the United States of America

TO

THE MEMORY OF

MY FATHER

PREFACE

The following discussion of the social character of the Christian churches is intended to be a practical contribution to the ethical problem of denominationalism. The writer cannot pretend to qualify either as a church historian or as a sociologist but he has sought to make an amateur's acquaintance with these subjects fruitful for the understanding of a difficult situation. The present work is the outcome of a course in "Symbolics" which the author was called upon to teach some years ago. The effort to distinguish churches primarily by reference to their doctrine and to approach the problem of church unity from a purely theological point of view appeared to him to be a procedure so artificial and fruitless that he found himself compelled to turn from theology to history, sociology, and ethics for a more satisfactory account of denominational differences and a more significant approach to the question of union.

The indebtedness of these chapters to Troeltsch, Weber, Tawney, Harnack, Mueller, and Gooch is even greater than can be indicated in precise references and will be readily recognized by those readers who are familiar with the works of these historians and economists. Among those to whom the author is especially obligated for advice, encouragement, and practical help are his wife, his sister, his former colleagues, Professors Paul N. Crusius and T. W.

Mueller of Elmhurst College, and, above all, his brother, Reinhold Niebuhr, without whose constant interest these pages would scarcely have been completed.

H. R. N.

October, 1929.

CONTENTS

The Social Sources of
Denominationalism

CHAPTER ONE

THE ETHICAL FAILURE OF THE DIVIDED CHURCH

I

Christendom has often achieved apparent success by ignoring the precepts of its founder. The church, as an organization interested in self-preservation and in the gain of power, has sometimes found the counsel of the Cross quite as inexpedient as have national and economic groups. In dealing with such major social evils as war, slavery, and social inequality, it has discovered convenient ambiguities in the letter of the Gospels which enabled it to violate their spirit and to ally itself with the prestige and power those evils had gained in their corporate organization. In adapting itself to the conditions of a civilization which its founder had bidden it to permeate with the spirit of divine love, it found that it was easier to give to Cæsar the things belonging to Cæsar if the examination of what might belong to God were not too closely pressed.

This proneness toward compromise which characterizes the whole history of the church, is no more difficult to understand than is the similar and inevitable tendency by which each individual Christian adapts the demands of the gospel to the necessities of existence in the body and in civilized society. It has often been pointed out that no ideal can be incorporated without the loss of some of its ideal character. When liberty gains a constitution, liberty is compromised; when fraternity elects officers, fraternity yields some of the ideal qualities of brotherhood to the necessities of government. And the gospel of Christ is especially subject to this sacrifice of character in the interest of organic embodiment; for the very essence of Christianity lies in the tension which it presupposes or creates between the worlds of nature and of spirit, and in its resolution of that conflict by means of justifying faith. It demands the impossible in conduct and belief; it runs counter to the instinctive life of man and exalts the rationality of the irrational; in a world of relativity it calls for unyielding loyalty to unchangeable absolutes. Clothe its faith in terms of philosophy, whether medieval or modern, and you lose the meaning of its high desires, of its living experience, reducing these to a set of opinions often irrelevant, sometimes contrary, to the original content. Organize its ethics—as organize them you must whenever two or three are gathered in the name of Christ—and the free spirit of forgiving love becomes a new law, requiring interpretation, commentary, and all the machinery of justice— just the sort of impersonal relationship which the gospel denies and combats. Place this society in the world, demanding that it be not of the world, and strenuous as may be its efforts to transcend or to sublimate the mundane life, it will yet be unable to escape all taint of conspiracy and connivance with the worldly interests it despises. Yet, on the other hand, Christian ethics will not permit a world-fleeing asceticism which seeks purity at the cost of service. At the end, if not at the beginning, of every effort to incorporate Christianity there is, therefore, a compromise, and the Christian cannot escape the necessity of seeking the last source of righteousness outside himself and the world in the divine aggression, in a justification that is by faith.

The fact that compromise is inevitable does not make it less an evil. The fault of every concession, of course, is that it is made too soon, before the ultimate resistance "to the blood" has been offered. Even where resistance seems to have gone to the uttermost the loyal man remembers that it might have been begun earlier, that it might have been continued a little longer, and that any compromise of the absolute good remains an evil. At last men must continue to condemn themselves not only for their failure to do what they could, but also for their failure to perform what they could not, for their denial of the absolute good whose categorical demands were laid upon their incapable will. But compromises are doubly evil when they are unacknowledged, when the emasculation of the Christian ideal remains undiscovered and when, in consequence, men take pride, as in an achievement, in a defeat of the essential gospel. Such unconscious hypocrisy not only bars the way to continued efforts to penetrate the stubborn stuff of life with the ethics of Jesus but is the author of further compromises made all too early. So it produces at last a spurious gospel unaware of its departure from the faith once delivered to the saints.

Denominationalism in the Christian church is such an unacknowledged hypocrisy. It is a compromise, made far too lightly, between Christianity and the world. Yet it often regards itself as a Christian achievement and glorifies its martyrs as bearers of the Cross. It represents the accommodation of Christianity to the caste-system of human society. It carries over into the organization of the Christian principle of brotherhood the prides and prejudices, the privilege and prestige, as well as the humiliations and abasements, the injustices and inequalities of that specious order of high and low wherein men find the satisfaction of their craving for vainglory. The division of the churches closely follows the division of men into the castes of national, racial, and economic groups. It draws the color line in the church of God; it fosters the misunderstandings, the self-exaltations, the hatreds of jingoistic nationalism by continuing in the body of Christ the spurious differences of provincial loyalties; it seats the rich and poor apart at the table of the Lord, where the fortunate may enjoy the bounty they have provided while the others feed upon the crusts their poverty affords.

II

The gospel's condemnation of divisiveness among men is one of its most characteristic and appealing elements. The spirit of Jesus revolted against Jewish class distinctions between the righteous few and the unhallowed many. He spoke to the outcast poor of the promise of the kingdom; he saw the typical child of God in a Samaritan who knew the meaning of human solidarity; ignoring the nationalism of Jews and Romans, he found faith superior to that of the chosen people in the heart of a centurion and sought his nation's glory in the rôle of a suffering servant. The ideal which was implicit in Jesus' teaching became explicit in Paul. Not only did this apostle refuse to recognize the religious differences between the parties of Peter, Apollos, Paul, and Christ, but—what is more important—he showed his converts that in Christ there can be neither Jew nor Greek, male nor female, bond nor free, and that with God there "is no respect of persons." Recognizing the diversity of gifts he resisted the ever-present tendency to find in diversity the excuse of division and he set forth that splendid theory of organic unity which remains for all time the ideal constitution of Christian society.[1] In James the spirit of equality in Christ again meets us in all his hearty condemnation of those who continue to observe in the service of the Lord those distinctions between rich and poor in which the world delights. The great Ephesian interpreter of the gospel recognized in Christ not only the divine Logos which informs the world with order but also the Son who is both child and brother, whose deep desire it is "that they may all be one," and the central meaning of whose teaching is interpretable only in the terms of sacrificing love.[2]

At this point, especially, the teaching of early Christianity met the wisdom of Stoic philosophers and the cosmopolitanism of the Roman world. The ideal became effective in the new church while it began slowly to penetrate into the social structure of the empire as a whole. The religious communism of the Jerusalem church, its surrender at the critical council of that stubborn sense of caste which barred the way to brotherhood between Jewish and Gentile Christians, the new attitude toward slaves expressed in the letter to Philemon and in the election of slaves to high office in Christian congregations, the sense of solidarity and equality which united masters and slaves and made Gentile disciples sacrifice their meager savings for the saints in Jewish Jerusalem, the communion meal itself with its lofty symbolism and its practical efficacy in overcoming the divisions of men—all these spoke of the reality of fellowship in Christ.[3]

Modern Christianity has returned with great enthusiasm to the study of this spirit and of these ideals of brotherhood. It has professed to find in them the solution of the difficulties and dangers of modern social life. The inequality of privilege in the economic order appears to the church to contain a fundamental denial of the Christian principle of brotherhood and to be symptomatic of an unhealthful state of society because it is contrary to the divine law inherent in the process of life as well as explicit in the gospel of Jesus. Nationalistic policies with

their self-centered attitudes and their inevitable fric-
tions, which culminate again and again in the bes-
tiality of war—these also are subject to the church's
strictures for all their cynical disregard of the Christian ethics and their appeal to the long-fostered
sentiments of pride in one's own and contempt for
another's national genius. The prejudice of racial
caste-systems expressed on the one hand in the exclusion of Orientals from the privileges enjoyed by Oc-
cidental racial groups and in the social and political
disabilities of the Negro, on the other hand in the ful-
some praise of the superior qualities of Nordic tribes,
seems no less contrary to the ideals of the Nazarene
and to the spirit of the community he founded.

But a skeptic world notes with amusement where
it is irreverent and with despair where it longs for a
saving word, that the organization which is loudest
in its praise of brotherhood and most critical of race
and class discriminations in other spheres is the most
disunited group of all, nurturing in its own structure
that same spirit of division which it condemns in
other relations. The world remembers that the idyllic
unity of early Christianity was of but short dura-
tion: that Jewish and Gentile Christians, even in the
days of Paul, often found their disagreements more
significant than their agreements, their sense of race
more potent than their sense of Christian solidarity.
It recalls that Ebionites, Monarchians, Arians, Nes-
torians, and Monophysites were flung off, despised,
and persecuted by the church in its great centripetal
movement toward Catholicism. It notes that East

[9]

and West and South and North, Slav and Latin and Teuton, have parted the garment of Christianity among them, unable to clothe a single body of Christ with the seamless vesture of his spirit. It sees the Orthodox church of the East maintaining a specious unity by recognizing everywhere the national principle in the organization of Hellenic, Russian, Cyprian, Serbian, Rumanian, Bulgarian, and other virtually independent groups which do not even share a common name and which, in time of war at least, subject the principles of Jesus to the ethics of nationalism. The Catholicism of Latin Christianity, it appears, has made its politic adjustment to classes and nationalities and, more successfully than other representatives of the gospel, preserves unity in the bond of peace; but it does so by governmental more than by spiritual means; in times of crisis it shows itself pliant to the incessant demands of nationality and class; and it continues to suffer from the results of that great failure when its Roman-Italian heritage and interest showed themselves more powerful than its Christian ideal. If the attention is directed to the North and the West, to the successors of the Reformation, the surrender of Christianity to national, racial, and economic caste-systems becomes even more apparent. Here the ideal of brotherhood has not only yielded to the principle of nationalism but has suffered the latter to exploit it in the interests of parties and of rulers until at times the church has become a mere appendage of the state. Here Lutheranism is divided into German, Danish, Swedish, and Norwegian groups, while Calvinism observes the national boundaries in the organization of Swiss, French, German, Dutch, Scotch, and English churches. Here the races confess the same creeds, engage in the same forms of worship, nurture the same hopes, but do so in divided churches, where white and black find it easier to confess than to practice their common sonship to God. Here rich and poor meet in their separate cathedrals and conventicles that each may achieve salvation in his own way and that their class loyalties may not be violated by the practice of the ethics they profess.

Once Parthians and Medes and Elamites, Cretans and Arabians, the dwellers in Mesopotamia, in Judea and Cappadocia, Pontus and Asia, heard the common language of the gospel with a common joy. Now they and their modern heirs are without a common language; the joy of the great community has been lost in the bickerings, rivalries, and misunderstandings of divided sects. The accord of Pentecost has resolved itself into a Babel of confused sounds; while devout men and women continue devoutly to confess, Sunday by Sunday, "I believe in one, holy, catholic Church."

III

The orthodox explanation of this strange phenomenon in the church of brotherhood has been sought in the divergence of opinion between men as to the manner of their soul's salvation. That strange interpretation of the faith which has prevailed since the days when Greek disputants carried into it the problems and the methods of Greek philosophy, and which professes to believe that the salvation of men and nations is dependent on the maintenance of some opinion about metaphysical processes, has been responsible for many false analyses of the character and mission of Christianity. This typically Greek evaluation of the nature and function of ideas must be held in part accountable for the intolerance in religion which has given rise to many denominations through the exclusion of groups professing an opinion more or less divergent from that which had become established. But it is also responsible for obscuring the fundamental ethical problems of denominationalism by regarding all differences from a purely ideological point of view.

The orthodox interpretation of denominationalism in Christianity looks upon the official creeds of the churches as containing the explanation of the sources and of the character of the prevailing differences. Roman Catholics are defined, from this point of view, as Christians who hold to a semi-Pelagian view of sin and grace, believe in the innately effective character of the sacraments, recognize the primacy of the Roman bishop and hold to other cognate principles of faith and practice. Lutherans are distinguished, the interpreter of the creed tells us, by their belief in justification by faith alone, by their exaltation of the word of God as the primary means of grace, and by their profession of the priesthood of all believers. The Calvinist is marked by his views on predestination, on the legal character of the Bible, and on church discipline. Baptists are members of their denomination because they are convinced that believers' baptism by immersion is alone justifiable. Methodists are what they are because they temper an underlying Calvinism by Arminian modifications. As for the many sub-groups to be found among Lutherans, Calvinists, Baptists, Methodists, these also vary from each other on one or another point of doctrine, which, it is said, explains their division and accounts for their antagonism. This mode of explanation has been popular since the time when Josephus described the Pharisees as a school of philosophers who maintained belief in the resurrection from the dead and in oral tradition, while the Sadducees were defined as those who held the opposite doctrines. The inadequacy of the explanation in this instance is patent. Certainly the Sadducees were not distinguished from the mass of Jewish people, or from the Pharisees, primarily by any religious opinions they held or failed to hold but by their social character as the members of the Hellenistic aristocracy; while back of Pharisaic ideas one looks for the fundamental element, for the racial loyalty which had its source in resistance to the Seleucid attempts to Hellenize Jewish civilization. Differences of opinion were surely present between Pharisees and Sadducees, but these differences had their roots in more profound social divergences. So it is with the Christian sects.

It is not possible to reduce all religious opinions and ideas to the category of rationalization, that is, to explain them as results of the universal human tendency to find respectable reasons for a practice desired from motives quite independent of the reasons urged. The psychology which regards all intellectual activity as such a rationalizing process is too patently one-sided to be able to maintain itself in the long run. Yet it is no less evident that much opinion or belief is in fact mere rationalization and that the reasons advanced for pursuing a given course of action are often far removed from the inspiring motive. This is true of many a political platform; it is true also of many a theological opinion. Again, many ideas which cannot be defined as rationalizations in the sense described are yet evidently secondary in character, representing the intellectual reflection of more fundamental social and cultural as well as religious conditions. An evident illustration of this relationship of ideas to underlying social conditions may be found in the attitude of Christians toward such institutions as private property, democracy, and slavery. Advancing and defending their positions on the basis of proof-texts drawn from the Scriptures, it has been possible for various sects to take antithetical views of the Christian or un-Christian character of these institutions. Only the purest novice in history will seek the explanation of such opinions in the proof-texts from which they purport to derive. In a similar fashion opinions as to church polity, varying from denomination to denomination, have been based in theory on New Testament reports of primitive church organization. The episcopal, the presbyterian, and the congregational forms have each been set forth as representing the original and ideal constitution of the Christian church. Yet the relationship of these forms to the political experience and desire of various groups is considerably more pertinent than is their relationship to the New Testament. Under the social and political conditions of the American frontier English presbyterianism, which had been convinced of its fidelity to the New Testament model, was almost unconsciously transformed into New England congregationalism, which now defended its form of organization as following the original and rightful Christian order. Episcopalianism was defended and attacked at many points in history, ostensibly because of its alleged maintenance of or departure from New Testament forms of church administration, but in reality because of its relationship to monarchical and absolute political government. The exaltation of the presbyter as the chief officer of the church, the endless quarrels as to the relative value of presbyterial and episcopal forms of polity, were supported by painstaking inquiries into the New Testament, by laborious definitions of Greek terms, by patient researches into the duties of non-Christian officials, who bore these titles before the church adopted the terminology. But the passionate conviction of the Calvinists that their form of organization was the right one had other sources than the savants' definitions of the meaning of "episcopos" or "presbyteros" in the Greek New Testament.

What is true of ethics and polity is true of theology. Less directly, but none the less effectively, theological opinions have their roots in the relationship of the religious life to the cultural and political conditions prevailing in any group of Christians. This does not mean that an economic or purely political interpretation of theology is justified, but it does mean that the religious life is so interwoven with social circumstances that the formulation of theology is necessarily conditioned by these. Where theology is regarded only from the ideological point of view, sight is lost of those very conditions which influence the divergence of its forms, and differences are explained on a speciously intellectual basis without taking into account the fundamental reasons for such variations. It is generally conceded that the theology of the first five centuries can be understood only if the psychology of the Greek mind and the social, religious, political, and economic conditions of the Roman empire are apprehended in their relationship to the new faith. One will fail completely to understand Roman Catholicism if one blinds one's eyes to the influence of the Latin spirit and of the institutions of the Cæsars upon its conception of Christianity and its formulation of doctrine. The spirit and the doctrines of Lutheranism derive not only from the New Testament but also from Luther's German temperament and from the political conditions of the church in Germany. Calvinism was no less influenced in its temper and theology by national character and by the interests of the economic class to which it especially appealed. Back of the divergences of doctrine one must look for the conditions which make now the one, now the other interpretation appear more reasonable or, at least, more desirable. Regarding theology from this point of view one will discover how the exigencies of church discipline, the demands of the national psychology, the effect of social tradition, the influence of cultural heritage, and the weight of economic interest play their rôle in the definition of religious truth. The importance of such elements is now generally recognized when the history of nations is under discussion. It is too often disregarded when denominational histories are written or sectarian differences investigated.[4]

IV

One element in the social sources of theological differentiation deserves especial attention. Max Weber and Ernst Troeltsch [5] have demonstrated how important are the differences in the sociological structure of religious groups in the determination of their doctrine. The primary distinction to be made here is that between the church and the sect, of which the former is a natural social group akin to the family or the nation while the latter is a voluntary association. The difference has been well described as lying primarily in the fact that members are born into the church while they must join the sect. Churches are inclusive institutions, frequently are national in scope, and emphasize the universalism of the gospel; while sects are exclusive in character, appeal to the individualistic element in Christianity, and emphasize its ethical demands. Membership in a church is socially obligatory, the necessary consequence of birth into a family or nation, and no special requirements condition its privileges; the sect, on the other hand, is likely to demand some definite type of religious experience as a pre-requisite of membership.

These differences in structure have their corollaries in differences in ethics and doctrine. The institutional church naturally attaches a high importance to the means of grace which it administers, to the system of doctrine which it has formulated, and to the official administration of sacraments and teaching by an official clergy; for it is an educational institution which must seek to train its youthful members to conformity in thought and practice and so fit them for the exercise of rights they have inherited. The associational sect, on the other hand, attaches primary importance to the religious experience of its members prior to their fellowship with the group, to the priesthood of all believers, to the sacraments as symbols of fellowship and pledges of allegiance. It frequently rejects an official clergy, preferring to trust for guidance to lay inspiration rather than to theological or liturgical expertness. The church as an inclusive social group is closely allied with national, economic, and cultural interests; by the very nature of its constitution it is committed to the accommodation of its ethics to the ethics of civilization; it must represent the morality of the respectable majority, not of the heroic minority. The sect, however, is always a minority group, whose separatist and semi-ascetic attitude toward "the world" is re-enforced by the loyalty which persecution nurtures. It holds with tenacity to its interpretation of Christian ethics and prefers isolation to compromise. At times it refuses participation in the government, at times rejects war, at times seeks to sever as much as possible the bonds which tie it to the common life of industry and culture. So the sociological structure, while resting in part on a conception of Christianity, reacts upon that conception and re-enforces or modifies it. On the other hand the adoption of one or the other type of constitution is itself largely due to the social condition of those who form the sect or compose the church. In Protestant history the sect has ever been the child of an outcast minority, taking its rise in the religious revolts of the poor, of those who were without effective representation in church or state and who formed their conventicles of dissent in the only way open to them, on the democratic, associational pattern. The sociological character of sectarianism, however, is almost always modified in the course of time by the natural processes of birth and death, and on this change in structure changes in doctrine and ethics inevitably follow. By its very nature the sectarian type of organization is valid only for one generation. The children born to the voluntary members of the first generation begin to make the sect a church long before they have arrived at the years of discretion. For with their coming the sect must take on the character of an educational and disciplinary institution, with the purpose of bringing the new generation into conformity with ideals and customs which have become traditional. Rarely does a second generation hold the convictions it has inherited with a fervor equal to that of its fathers, who fashioned these convictions in the heat of conflict and at the risk of martyrdom. As generation succeeds generation, the isolation of the community from the world becomes more difficult. Furthermore, wealth frequently increases when the sect subjects itself to the discipline of asceticism in work and expenditure; with the increase of wealth the possibilities for culture also become more numerous and involvement in the economic life of the nation as a whole can less easily be limited. Compromise begins and the ethics of the sect approach the churchly type of morals. As with the ethics, so with the doctrine, so also with the administration of religion. An official clergy, theologically educated and schooled in the refinements of ritual, takes the place of lay leadership; easily imparted creeds are substituted for the difficult enthusiasms of the pioneers; children are born into the group and infant baptism or dedication becomes once more a means of grace. So the sect becomes a church.

Religious history amply illustrates the process. An outstanding example is the "Half-Way Covenant" of the New England churches, which provided for the baptism of the children of second-generation, unconverted parents who had "owned the covenant" and submitted to the discipline of the church without being able to attain full membership because of their lack of the experience of salvation. The rise of "birth-right membership" in the Society of Friends shows the same process at work while the histories of Mennonites, Baptists, and Methodists offer further illustrations. Doctrines and practice change with the mutations of social structure, not vice versa; the ideological interpretation of such changes quite misses the point.

v

The evils of denominationalism do not lie, however, in this differentiation of churches and sects. On the contrary, the rise of new sects to champion the uncompromising ethics of Jesus and "to preach the gospel to the poor" has again and again been the effective means of recalling Christendom to its mission. This phase of denominational history must be regarded as helpful, despite the break in unity which it brings about. The evil of denominationalism lies in the conditions which makes the rise of sects desirable and necessary: in the failure of the churches to transcend the social conditions which fashion them into caste-organizations, to sublimate their loyalties to standards and institutions only remotely relevant if not contrary to the Christian ideal, to resist the temptation of making their own self-preservation and extension the primary object of their endeavor.

The domination of class and self-preservative church ethics over the ethics of the gospel must be held responsible for much of the moral ineffectiveness of Christianity in the West. Not only or primarily because denominationalism divides and scatters the energies of Christendom, but more because its signalizes the defeat of the Christian ethics of brotherhood by the ethics of caste is it the source of Christendom's moral weakness. The ethical effectiveness of an individual depends on the integration of his character, on the synthesis of his values and desires into a system dominated by his highest good; the ethical effectiveness of a group is no less dependent on its control by a morale in which all subordinate purposes are organized around a leading ideal. And the churches are ineffective because they lack such a common morale.

The measure of their ethical weakness, of course, is taken especially in the crises, in wars and social revolutions. Divided against themselves they must leave the work of social construction to those forces which can develop an effective morale, which have for their basis the common and all too human interests in acquisition, in national and racial prestige, and which are unified by the common purposes and common fears of mankind at its lower levels. Under these circumstances it is almost inevitable that the churches should adopt the psychologically more effective morale of the national, racial, and economic groups with which they are allied. Hence they usually join in the "Hurrah" chorus of jingoism, to which they add the sanction of their own "Hallelujah"; and, through their adeptness at rationalization, they support the popular morale by persuading it of the nobility of its motives. The specifically

Christian ethics is allowed to fade into the background while the ethics of the social classes takes its place, unless, indeed, it is possible to re-interpret the Christian ideal in such a way that its complete accord with social morality is demonstrated.

The lack of an effective, common, Christian ethics in the churches is illustrated by the manner in which they have divided their loyalties in each national crisis in the history of America and allied themselves with the struggling partisans of parliament and marketplace. During the American Revolution the rector of Trinity Church, New York, wrote to an English confrere, "I have the pleasure to assure you that all the society's missionaries without excepting one, in New Jersey, New York, Connecticut, and, so far as I learn, in the other New England colonies, have proved themselves faithful, loyal subjects in these trying times; and have to the utmost of their power opposed the spirit of disaffection and rebellion which has involved this continent in the greatest calamities. I must add that all the other clergy of our church in the above colonies though not in the society's service, have observed the same line of conduct." On the other hand, he testifies, the Presbyterian ministers, with singular uniformity, are promoting by preaching and every other effort in their power "all the measures of the congress, however extravagant." [6] In any case, and this applies also to Congregationalists, Baptists, Methodists, and the other churches in the revolutionary colonies, one hears no word of a common Christian system of

[23]

values to which all can express allegiance. Each religious group gives expression to that code which forms the morale of the political or economic class it represents. They function as political and class institutions, not as Christian churches.

The case was not different in the slavery crisis. Methodism had carried an anti-slavery doctrine in its platform from the very beginning, but even White-field urged the desirability of eliminating from the charter of Georgia the prohibition of slavery and when Methodism became the church of the slave-holder as well as of the poor tradesman it soon divided into a Northern and a Southern branch although the gradual emasculation of the anti-slavery clause in the old program was designed to maintain peace at the expense of principle. So it was also with Baptists and Presbyterians. Again the interests of economic class bent to their will the ethics of the Christian church and it was unable to speak a certain word on the issue of slavery. When the irrepressible conflict came the various denominations, as was to be expected, showed themselves to be the mouthpieces of the economic and sectional groups they represented.

The rôle played by the churches in the World War is too well known to require comment. Even when resistance was offered to war-time psychology it was often apparent that such resistance was not animated by Christian principles but by the social attitudes of immigrant groups, in whom the Old World heritage had not lost its force. Almost always and everywhere in modern times the churches have represented the ethics of classes and nations rather than a common and Christian morality. Evident as this is in the crises, it is no less true of the times between crises. In the issues of municipal and national elections, on the questions of industrial relationships, of the conservation or abrogation of social customs and institutions—including the prohibition issue—the denominations have been the religious spokesmen of the special non-religious groups with which they are allied.

For the denominations, churches, sects, are sociological groups whose principle of differentiation is to be sought in their conformity to the order of social classes and castes. It would not be true to affirm that the denominations are not religious groups with religious purposes, but it is true that they represent the accommodation of religion to the caste system. They are emblems, therefore, of the victory of the world over the church, of the secularization of Christianity, of the church's sanction of that divisiveness which the church's gospel condemns.

Denominationalism thus represents the moral failure of Christianity. And unless the ethics of brotherhood can gain the victory over this divisiveness within the body of Christ it is useless to expect it to be victorious in the world. But before the church can hope to overcome its fatal division it must learn to recognize and to acknowledge the secular character of its denominationalism.

CHAPTER TWO

THE CHURCHES OF THE DISINHERITED

One phase of denominationalism is largely explicable by means of a modified economic interpretation of religious history; for the divisions of the church have been occasioned more frequently by the direct and indirect operation of economic factors than by the influence of any other major interest of man. Furthermore, it is evident that economic stratification is often responsible for maintaining divisions which were originally due to differences of another sort. Social history demonstrates how a racial class may retain its solidarity and distinction by becoming an economic class, and religious history offers examples of churches which were originally racial in character but maintained their separateness under new conditions because the racial group developed into an economic entity. It is true, of course, in this case as in that of others, that no one element, the religious or the economic or the racial, operates alone. Economic classes tend to take on a cultural character and economic differences between groups result in educational and psychological distinctions between them. The interaction of the various factors is well exemplified in the history of immigrant groups in the United States. These are distinguished at first by racial or national character, but they are usually also the lowest groups in the economic and cultural scale during the first generation and, therefore, their distinction from other groups is triply fortified. Their churches, as a result, are distinguished economically and culturally as well as racially from the denominations of previous immigrants who have risen in the economic scale while losing their specifically national or racial character.

An exclusively economic interpretation of denominationalism would, because of this interaction, be as erroneous as the exclusively economic interpretation of political history is bound to be. It is quite unjustifiable, above all, to leave the religious factor itself out of account in dealing with religious movements. Only because the inspiration of such movements is religious do they develop the tremendous energy they display in history. Yet an exclusively religious interpretation, especially a doctrinal one, is likely to miss the point of the whole development even more completely than does an exclusively economic explanation. For if religion supplies the energy, the goal, and the motive of sectarian movements, social factors no less decidedly supply the occasion, and determine the form the religious dynamic will take. Were spiritual energies to develop unchecked they would scarcely issue in the formation of such denominations as now compose Christianity. Religious energies are dammed up, confined to narrow channels, split into parallel streams, by the non-religious distinctions and classifications of

Christians. The source of a religious movement, therefore, need not be economic for its results to take on a definitely economic character. On the other hand, economic conditions may supply the occasion for the rise of a new religious movement without determining its religious value. In any case, however, the character of the denomination issuing from the movement is explicable only if the influence of economic factors be taken into consideration.

So regarded, one phase of the history of denominationalism reveals itself as the story of the religiously neglected poor, who fashion a new type of Christianity which corresponds to their distinctive needs, who rise in the economic scale under the influence of religious discipline, and who, in the midst of a freshly acquired cultural respectability, neglect the new poor succeeding them on the lower plane. This pattern recurs with remarkable regularity in the history of Christianity. Anabaptists, Quakers, Methodists, Salvation Army, and more recent sects of like type illustrate this rise and progress of the churches of the disinherited.

Not only the religious revolutions of the poor, however, have left their impress on the denominational history of Christendom. One may also speak with G. K. Chesterton of the revolt of the rich against the poor. Some of the earlier churches of the Reformation received much of their specific character from their alliance with rising commercialism and set forth an interpretation of Christianity conformable with their major economic interests. To this group belong especially the Calvinistic churches, as has been shown by Weber, Cunningham, and Tawney.[1] Other sects, whose origins are not so readily identifiable with economic movements, have preserved their separate character because of the economic status of their members and are distinguished from their sister denominations less by doctrine than by their wealth and the consequent conservatism of ethics and thought.

I

That astute historian of the social ethics of the churches, Ernst Troeltsch, once wrote: "The really creative, church-forming, religious movements are the work of the lower strata. Here only can one find that union of unimpaired imagination, simplicity in emotional life, unreflective character of thought, spontaneity of energy and vehement force of need, out of which an unconditioned faith in a divine revelation, the naïveté of complete surrender and the intransigence of certitude can rise. Need upon the one hand and the absence of an all-relativizing culture of reflection on the other hand are at home only in these strata. All great community-building revelations have come forth again and again out of such circles and the significance and power for further development in such religious movements have always been dependent upon the force of the original impetus given in such naïve revelations as well as on the energy of the conviction which made this impetus absolute and divine." [2] This passage not only describes the character of the religious movements which originate in the culturally lower strata of society but also indicates wherein the religious expatriation of these classes consists and shows the dialectic of the process which gives rise to ever new movements.

The religion of the untutored and economically disfranchised classes has distinct ethical and psychological characteristics, corresponding to the needs of these groups. Emotional fervor is one common mark. Where the power of abstract thought has not been highly developed and where inhibitions on emotional expression have not been set up by a system of polite conventions, religion must and will express itself in emotional terms. Under these circumstances spontaneity and energy of religious feeling rather than conformity to an abstract creed are regarded as the tests of religious genuineness. Hence also the formality of ritual is displaced in such groups by an informality which gives opportunity for the expression of emotional faith and for a simple, often crude, symbolism. An intellectually trained and liturgically minded clergy is rejected in favor of lay leaders who serve the emotional needs of this religion more adequately and who, on the other hand, are not allied by culture and interest with those ruling classes whose superior manner of life is too obviously purchased at the expense of the poor.

Ethically, as well as psychologically, such religion bears a distinct character. The salvation which it seeks and sets forth is the salvation of the socially disinherited. Intellectual naïveté and practical need combine to create a marked propensity toward millenarianism, with its promise of tangible goods and of the reversal of all present social systems of rank. From the first century onward, apocalypticism has always been most at home among the disinherited. The same combination of need and social experience brings forth in these classes a deeper appreciation of the radical character of the ethics of the gospel and greater resistance to the tendency to compromise with the morality of power than is found among their more fortunate brethren. Again, the religion of the poor is characterized by the exaltation of the typical virtues of the class and by the apprehension under the influence of the gospel of the moral values resident in its necessities. Hence one finds here, more than elsewhere, appreciation of the religious worth of solidarity and equality, of sympathy and mutual aid, of rigorous honesty in matters of debt, and the religious evaluation of simplicity in dress and manner, of the wisdom hidden to the wise and prudent but revealed to babes, of poverty of spirit, of humility and meekness. Simple and direct in its apprehension of the faith, the religion of the poor shuns the relativizations of ethical and intellectual sophistication and by its fruits in conduct often demonstrates its moral and religious superiority.

Whenever Christianity has become the religion of the fortunate and cultured and has grown philosophical, abstract, formal, and ethically harmless in the process, the lower strata of society find themselves religiously expatriated by a faith which neither meets their psychological needs nor sets forth an appealing ethical ideal. In such a situation the right leader finds little difficulty in launching a new movement which will, as a rule, give rise to a new denomination. When, however, the religious leader does not appear and religion remains bound in the forms of middle-class culture, the secularization of the masses and the transfer of their religious fervor to secular movements, which hold some promise of salvation from the evils that afflict them, is the probable result.

The development of the religion of the disinherited is illustrated not only by the history of various sects in Christianity but by the rise of that faith itself. It began as a religion of the poor, of those who had been denied a stake in contemporary civilization. It was not a socialist movement, as some have sought to show, but a religious revolution, centering in no mundane Paradise but in the cult of Christ.[3] Yet it was addressed to the poor in the land, to fishermen and peasants, to publicans and outcasts. In Corinth as in Galilee, in Rome as in Antioch, not many "wise after the flesh, not many mighty, not many noble were called"; and this condition continued far down into the third century. Origen and Tertullian as well as the opponents of Christianity, notably Celsus, bear ample testimony to the fact that "the uneducated are always in a majority with us."[4] But the new faith became the religion of the cultured, of the rulers, of the sophisticated; it lost its spontaneous energy amid the quibblings of abstract theologies; it sacrificed its ethical rigorousness in compromise with the policies of governments and nobilities; it abandoned its apocalyptic hopes as irrelevant to the well-being of a successful church. Now began the successive waves of religious revolution, the constant recrudescences of religions of the poor who sought an emotionally and ethically more satisfying faith than was the metaphysical and formal cult Christianity had come to be. Montanism, the Franciscan movement, Lollardy, Waldensianism, and many similar tendencies are intelligible only as the efforts of the religiously disinherited to discover again the sources of effective faith. Yet on the whole it is true that the Roman Church, with its ritual, its pageantry, and its authoritative doctrine, supplied to the unsophisticated groups a type of religion which largely satisfied their longings; for under the necessity of adapting itself to the inundation of the northern tribes it had evolved a system of leadership and worship congenial to the naïve mind and had learned to set forth salvation in terms not abstract but tangible and real though remote. The Roman Church, despite the evident failings of scholasticism and papal policy and sacerdotal luxury, was unable to maintain its integrity not so much because it did not meet the needs of the lower strata as because it did not sufficiently accommodate itself to the new middle classes represented by humanism, the new capitalism and nationalism, as well as for reasons not primarily connected with the economic and cultural stratification of society.

II

The failure of the Reformation to meet the religious needs of peasants and other disfranchised groups is a chapter writ large in history. With all of its native religious fervor it remained the religion of the middle classes and the nobility. The Peasants' War and the Anabaptist movement were the result; for distinct as these two movements were, their close relationships are evident in history. Thomas Muenzer, the arch-enemy of Luther, was Anabaptist as well as revolutionary leader. The Zwickau prophets and Melchior Hoffmann represented the political and economic as well as the religious interests of the poor in proclaiming a faith which promised not only the salvation of emotional experience wherein the believer transcended the problems of a toilsome, humdrum life, but also gave assurance of deliverance from political and social oppressions through the establishment of Christ's perfect brotherhood.[5]

Honestly and naïvely the peasants of Germany had believed that Luther's appeal to the New Testament was an appeal not to Pauline theology alone but to the ethics of the Sermon on the Mount as well. All too soon they discovered that the new Protestantism they had espoused so heartily protested less against their masters than against their masters' enemies and that the new faith dealt with their extreme necessities even less effectively than did the old. The priesthood of all believers, they found, meant deliverance neither from the abstruseness of dogma and the formality of sacramentalism nor from the inequalities of political and economic ethics. From Luther they learned that they could not look to Protestantism for salvation from the dual standard which bade rulers rule in accordance with the code of Old Testament precepts of strict reward and punishment while it required subjects to obey their political and economic masters in the spirit of a Christian and self-sacrificing meekness. Had not Luther said to them, "Listen, dear Christians, to your Christian right. Thus speaks your supreme Lord Christ, whose name you bear: Ye shall not resist evil, but whosoever shall compel thee to go one mile, go with him two, and if any would take away thy coat, let him have thy cloak also, and whosoever smiteth thee on thy right cheek, turn to him the other also. Do you hear, you Christian congregation? How does your project agree with this right? You will not bear that anyone inflict evil or injustice upon you, but want to be free and suffer only complete goodness and justice. . . . If you do not want to bear such a right, then you had better put away the Christian name and boast of another name in accordance with your deeds, or Christ himself will snatch his name away from you, so that it will be too hard for you to bear." [6] But not long thereafter this same Luther had addressed their masters in other terms in his pamphlet "Against the Thieving and Murderous Hordes of Peasants"—a production which has well been called a "disgrace to literature, to say nothing of religion." "Dear masters," he wrote in this pamphlet, "deliver here, save

here, help here, have mercy upon the poor people.
Stab, hit, kill here, whoever can; and though you die
in this, happy are you, for a more blessed death you
can never find; for you die in obedience to the
divine word and command (Romans 13) and in the
service of love, to save your neighbor from the bonds
of hell and devil." "Here let whoever can give
blows, strangle, stab—secretly or openly—and remember that nothing can be more poisonous, harmful,
and devilish than a revolutionary; just as one must
kill a mad dog, for if you do not slay him he will slay
you and a whole land with you." All of this, it is
true, Luther justified by ample appeal not to the
Old Testament but to the New. "It does not help the
peasants," he wrote, "that they claim that in Genesis
I and II all things were created free and common
and that we have all been equally baptized. For in
the New Testament Moses counts for nothing, but
there stands our Master Christ and casts us with
body and possessions under the Kaiser's and worldly
law when he says, 'Give to Cæsar the things that are
Cæsar's.'" [7] So the disinherited were ruled out of
Protestantism and discovered their last estate to be
worse than the former, for the dualism of Catholic
social ethics had been in favor of a spiritual, not
primarily of a political and economic, aristocracy,
while the new faith proclaimed that "the ass will have
blows and the people will be ruled by force." [8] Thus,
in the very first years of the new movement the
tendency toward cleavage along economic lines, so
baneful for all later Protestantism, came to expres-

sion. "As the poor found their spiritual needs best supplied in the conventicle of dissent, official Lutheranism became an established church, predominantly an aristocratic and middle-class party of vested interest and privilege." [9]

The Swiss Reformation resulted in the same division between the Christianity of the bourgeoisie and that of the poor. In fact it was in Zurich that the representatives of the new emotional and social religion had first appeared. There they had met, after an early friendship with Zwingli, that reformer's rebuff, for "the humanist could have little sympathy with an uncultured and ignorant group—such they were, in spite of the fact that a few leaders were university graduates—and the statesman could not admit in his categories a purpose that was sectarian as against the state church and democratic as against the existing aristocracy." [10] Accused of communism, which Zwingli considered a sin in the light of a divine sanction of private property implied in the sixth commandment, the leaders of the Protestantism of the poor were fined, banished, and, in some instances, executed.

In the Netherlands, in Poland, in England, at last in America also, the Anabaptists met a similar fate and the expatriation of the poor and uneducated from the new church went on with violence and much shedding of blood. Neither Lutheranism nor Calvinism had a message for them and both resented, with the vehemence of those whose economic rather than religious interests are threatened, the attempt to found a religion which met the need for a Christianity of emotional fervor and for a social reconstruction.

Under such circumstances the rise of the first Protestant sect, as distinct from the churches of the Reformation, took place. "It was a movement," as Bax points out, "constituted in the main of the disinherited classes of the time, the peasants, the poorer handicraftsmen, and the journeymen of the towns, to whose oppressed position, economically and politically, it powerfully appealed." [11] Its ethical interests came into appearance not only in the early revolutionary movements but even more in the later practice of pacific and non-resistant morality, in the rejection of the oath, in the refusal to participate in warfare and in government, in the practice of equality and mutual aid as well as in the frequent communism of individual groups. Its religious character was made evident in the insistence on voluntary membership, on adult baptism of the converted, in the democratic election and ordination of pastors by local churches, in lay preaching and congregational organization, and especially in the phenomena of revivalism. Persecuted vindictively on the continent and lacking adequate leadership, Anabaptism all but disappeared there leaving the peoples who had been disappointed by the failure readier for the message of the old Catholicism than for that of the new Protestantism. A remnant was gathered by Menno Simons, founder of the now much divided Mennonites. But with Simons began also the inevitable tendency accompanying the rise of a religious group in fortune and culture—the tendency toward a relaxation of the ethical demand and toward formalization of the cult. From violent revolution the path of development led through stubborn non-resistance and unyielding assertion by non-assertion of the principles of equality and love to an accommodating quietism. The Anabaptists, however, were too broken by the Protestant Inquisition to become a strong church, affiliated with wealth and prestige. Isolated by persecution, as the Jews had been isolated, they formed a narrow sect, cut off from other churches not only by the caste-consciousness of early Lutherans and Calvinists but by their own social loyalties to their outcast group. A splendid devotion to principles remains among many of the heirs of the sixteenth-century prophets to the disinherited, but even more effective is the consciousness of kind. And that is another phase of the tragedy of caste in the church of Christ, for castes make outcasts and outcasts form castes.

III

In seventeenth-century England as in sixteenth-century Germany a church of the poor came into being to meet the needs an official and middle-class Reformation seemed incapable of supplying. Naturally not without some dependence on the Anabaptist movement, but more in response to a similar social and religious situation, Quakerism developed as the Anglo-Saxon parallel to Anabaptism.

The social disorders of early Edwardean days,

though connected in part with the Continental movement, were scarcely religious in character. The masses of the English people remained Catholic, for their needs, apparently, were adequately met by the ministrations of Roman ritualism and imagery; and when Catholicism waned, in Elizabeth's reign, they found that the moderate reforms of the Anglican church did not deprive them of these satisfactions. But when the real Reformation occurred in England, when it raised the popular hopes for a thorough-going Christianization of society and then took on the typically middle-class and intellectual form of Puritanism, a religious revolt of the poor became inevitable.

Just as had been the case in Germany the party of the disinherited made common cause at first with the reformers, for here as there they expected, in the days before the character of the new movement became evident, that it would usher in those economic and political readjustments which they especially required. The cleavage between middle-class and proletarian reformations, nascent in the slow growth of the General Baptists from 1620 onward and in the early stages of Independency, became explicit in the time of Cromwell with the rise of Millenarians, Antinomians, Anabaptists, Seekers, Ranters, and, finally, Quakers.[12]

The relationship of the reformation movement among the disinherited to Presbyterianism and Congregationalism is especially instructive for the understanding of the character of the religion of the poor.

That Presbyterianism, from the very outset, failed to meet either the religious or the ethical needs of the people is evident. Like Calvinism everywhere it was suspicious of the common man. It is true that the teaching of the Genevan reformer supplied one of the main foundations for the development of modern democracy, but in the earlier centuries of Protestantism that leader's contempt for the rule of the people, shared by his disciples in England and Scotland, formed an effective barrier against the popular movement. McGiffert has pointed out that it was far from Calvin's intention to promote either civil liberty or democracy and that he was "at best only indirectly responsible for a development which he would have been entirely out of sympathy with had he lived to witness it." [13] The final chapter of the Institutes bears repeated witness to the reformer's love of the virtue of obedience on the part of the people and to his aversion to every type of revolutionary activity. "If we have this constantly present to our eyes and impressed upon our hearts," he writes, "that the most iniquitous kings are placed on their thrones by the same decree by which the authority of all kings is established, those seditious thoughts will never enter our minds, that a king is to be treated according to his merits, and that it is not reasonable for us to be subject to a king who does not on his part perform toward us those duties which his office requires." [14] Aristocratic as he was in his tendencies, he was followed in this by the English and even by the Scotch Presbyterians, by a Baillie who declares that "popular government bringeth in confusion, making the feet above the head" and by a Clement Walker who complains of the Independents that they "have cast all the mysteries and secrets of government before the vulgar." [15] The antagonism of English Presbyterianism to the monarchy was not at all based on democratic convictions but on the desire to substitute theocracy after the Genevan pattern for a too Catholic royal authority in matters of religion. When times changed and an anti-Presbyterian democracy raised its head in the army, Presbyterians quickly changed their tactics and "were all for the maintenance of the monarchy and were generally on the side of the gentry and the established order." [16] With its scanty respect for the common people and their causes, Presbyterianism united the rigorous Calvinistic discipline, designed to free men from the sins of luxury and sensuality rather than from the evils of injustice and inequality. Like its Genevan prototype it was without any real awareness of the social evils which oppressed the common people, while the sober kingdom of God on earth which it sought to found was not designed either to excite the hopes or to enlist the energies of those for whom temptation to luxurious living was, to say the least, an abstract and remote contingency.

In its intellectualism as in its ethics, Presbyterianism moved in a sphere far removed from the religious life and needs of the common people. What had the Westminster Confession and the learned discourses of the university-trained divines to do with the piety of craftsman and yeoman? If the untutored classes were to find reality in religion and were to appropriate it as a vital possession—as the pressure of the times bade them do—they needed a religious faith which could become immediate to them in emotion.[17] The abstract theological terminologies of Presbyterian confessions and sermons were not only unintelligible to them, they were irrelevant. The whole trend of the day was against any second-hand religion, handed down from above by constituted authority, whether political or theological, and from this point of view the new presbyter was "only the old priest writ large," as Milton remarked in another connection. Presbyterianism was intellectualistic, it was authoritarian, it was aristocratic; the disinherited required an emotionally experienceable and expressible faith, and one which contained some promise of social amelioration. Westminster could have no appeal for them. And so "the sects which had sprung forth like a harvest of armed men from the soil" threw themselves into opposition to the Presbyterians.[18]

The Puritanism of Independency seemed at first to offer a more adequate shelter to the poor. Brownists and Separatists in the waning sixteenth and early seventeenth centuries appeared, despite their Calvinism, to represent the religious needs and ethical desires of the religiously disinherited. The men and women who found their last refuge on the shores of Plymouth Bay were in the true apostolic succession; the simplicity and fervor of their piety were matched by the sincerity of their Christian brotherhood. Servants and common sailors signed the Mayflower compact along with Brewster and other "substantial citizens." Before the days of the Westminster Assembly, Independency "was spoken of with contempt because it numbered the poor and ignorant in its ranks." [19] In the New Model Army, Independency was the watchword around which rallied republicans and soldiers who hoped for Christ's kingdom. In 1645 Baxter, seeking to reform the Army in which "Independency and Anabaptistry extreamly prevail'd . . . and Antinomianism and Arminianism were equally distributed," found that the leaders who thought that "Providence would cast the Truth of Religion and the Kingdom upon them as Conquerors" were "generally men that had bin hatcht up in London among the old Separatists." [20] Independents and Anabaptists were coupled together as by Howells, who wrote in 1636, "If I hate any 'tis those that trouble the sweet peace of our church. I could be content to see an Anabaptist go to hell on a Brownist's back." [21]

But Independency did not remain the people's church. During the troublesome forties it had risen to power with Cromwell but by the early fifties it had lost its place as the dominant sect. "They had no so great congregations of the common people," Clarendon now wrote of them, "but were followed by the most substantial citizens." [22] Perhaps Independency had never been a true people's church. The fortunes of the day thrust leadership upon it and, between 1630 and 1650, caused soldiers and workers to look to it for redress and for the fulfilment of their Utopian hopes. Its principle of toleration had attracted to it sectaries of all sorts and these had forced republicanism upon it, but its espousal of this ideal was at first only half-hearted [23] and after a brief period of real democratic fervor it suffered, with its great genius Milton, the disillusionment of the discovery that the country of freemen it had dreamed of was an "inconsistent, irrational, and hapless herd, begotten to servility." [24] At all events it is true that Independency served merely as a halting place for the representatives of democratic religion and ethics on their passage from the church to the sectarian bodies, the Anabaptists, Millenarians, and Quakers.[25] In a short time the sectarian branch of Puritanism was scarcely distinguishable in social character from its churchly brother, Presbyterianism. "Then," as Tawney writes, "the splendours and illusions vanished; the force of common things prevailed; the metal cooled in the mould; and the Puritan spirit, shorn of its splendours and illusions, settled finally into its decent bed of equable respectability." [26]

So, at first in connection with Independency but later in opposition to it, the revolutionary churches of the poor took their rise. As in sixteenth-century Germany, conditions were conducive to such development. Poverty pressed more severely on the poor than ever. The hardships wrought by the enclosure acts, added to the chronic evil of rising prices—due to the discovery of new supplies of gold and silver and to the monopolies in many of the necessities of life—were now multiplied by the miseries of civil war, by the increase in taxation, and by a series of unusually bad harvests during the forties.[27] As in every people's war the sense of the individual worth of the common soldier and citizen was greatly heightened, not without effective aid from Presbyterianism and Independency. With the king out of the way and all established order in a state of flux, "all the people were in expectation." Utopia was in the air. The increasing common knowledge of the Scriptures, the influence of political and religious ideas drawn from Holland and America, contributed each their share to the situation. Ideas long current in the little conventicles of Familists and Baptists now became common property. Need and opportunity met once more to bring forth a Christianity of the disinherited. Anabaptists, Millenarians or Fifth Monarchy Men, Antinomians, Seekers, Ranters, Diggers, Levellers, and, last of all, the Quakers began to flourish.[28] The new spirit doubtless showed itself in some very uncouth forms, as Selbie points out, "but it belongs to the movement of the times and was the needed reaction against a religion of formalism." [29]

That it was a movement of the "poor and ignorant," all statements of the period testify. Its leaders were recruited almost wholly from the upper ranks of the least fortunate classes—craftsmen, cobblers, weavers, men with little Latin and less Greek, whose native emotionalism had not been inhibited by the formalism of classical learning and who had not been alienated from the common people by the association of education with special privilege. Lay preachers were so numerous and cobblers so frequently found among them that the Erastian Thomas Coleman, in a sermon to the House of Commons in 1645, expressed the opinion that if the tendency were not checked "the issue may be that one may bind his sonne prentice to a cobler and at seven years he may go out free a minister." [30] Gerald Winstanley, leader of the Diggers, had been a London tradesman; "beaten out of estate and trade," he said, by London's "cheating sons in the thieving art of buying and selling," he was "forced to live a country life where likewise with taxes and free quarter [his] weak back found the burden heavier than [he] could bear." [31] George Fox was a cobbler and the son of a weaver. Lilburne, leader of the Levellers, though the son of a gentleman, had been apprenticed in early youth to a London cloth-maker. Others, such as Naylor and Thomas Harrison, had started their careers in the ranks of the army. That there were also formally well educated men among the leaders, as in the Anabaptist movement on the Continent a century before, is not to be denied, but these were in the minority and not of great significance.

As were the leaders so were the rank and file. It was admitted by opponents that "men impoverished by long troubles must needs have great propensions to hearken to those that proclaim a golden age at hand, under the name of Christ and the saints." [32]

Of the Fifth Monarchy men under Harrison, the official reports stated that they were "a confluence of silly wretches" and that "the number and quality of the persons engaged were truly very inconsiderable and indeed despicable." [33]   The Quakers, said Pagitt in his *Heresiography*, were "made up of the dregs of the common people," [34] and one of the friendlier critics of the movement pointed out that it did the magistrates yeoman service in reclaiming such "as neither magistrate nor minister speak to." [35]

The stream of religious and political revolt was divided into numerous channels. Until George Fox came there was no leader great enough to define its banks and to give it direction. Like almost all such revolts of the disinherited it almost came to naught because of the lack of an adequate leadership to stop its extravagances and to guide its great dynamic. Crude and sometimes horrible excesses were discovered, to be exploited as the atrocities of the movement by its enemies and to alienate the sympathies of many friends. But in all of its ramifications and divisions there was a certain unity; two characteristics marked the religious social revolt from Diggers and Levellers to Quakers—the doctrine of inner experience as the source of authority and the common hope of Christ's kingdom on earth. These two major common characteristics implied other equally general but less important features, such as the sectarian organization, the rejection of professional clergy, and the dependence on lay preaching, the spiritualist interpretation of Scriptures, the rejection of the monarchy and the less frequent, but not rare, espousal of communism.

In Millenarianism, the special inspiration of Harrison and the Fifth Monarchy men but common to all the sects, the two tendencies toward emotional and individual religious experience and toward ethical and social reconstruction met. "Their prate," says Coke, of the Fifth Monarchy men, "was to make way for Christ's monarchy on earth." [36] This apocalypticism was combined with spiritualist, prophetic fervour. Visions, revelations, and illuminations are the natural accompaniment of such dynamic religious movements which receive fresh stimuli in this direction also from the example of primitive Christianity.[37] Winstanley, the Digger leader, was both mystic and communist. "Not a year since," he wrote, "my heart was filled with sweet thoughts and many things were revealed to me I never read in books nor heard from the mouth of flesh; and when I began to speak of them some people could not hear my words. Then I took my spade and began to dig on St. George's Hill." [38] Or again, "This Spirit of reason (the creative reason which is the divine Logos) is not without a man, but within every man; hence he need not run after others to tell him or to teach him; for this Spirit is his maker, he dwells in him and if his flesh were subject thereunto, he would daily find teaching therefrom, though he dwelt alone and saw the face of no other man." [39] Even the Levellers, political rather than religious party though they were, shared much of the religious character of the

sects.[40]   The Ranters "made it their business to set
up the Light of Nature under the name of Christ in
Men, and to dishonour and cry down the church,
Scriptures, Ministry, Worship and Ordinances; and
called men to hearken to the Christ within them."
The Seekers, says the same writer, taught that "the
Scriptures were uncertain . . . that our ministry
is null and void and without authority." [41]   The excesses of the time, Naylor's proclamation of himself
as the Christ, the frequent occurrences of prophesy-
ing by naked men and women parading through the
streets, Fox walking barefoot through the "bloody
city of Litchfield"—give evidence also of the spiritualist character of the movement.   The Quaker doctrine of the inner light was the final quiet precipitate
of this turbid emotionalism.   The priesthood of all
believers rather than the authority of the Scriptures
is the guiding principle here and the assurance of
salvation through immediate experience, not through
the mediation of priest and sacrament or word, is the
goal of religious endeavor.

The second characteristic of the movement was its
program of social reformation.   Its expectation of
the coming of the Kingdom of Christ had its solid
foundation in the physical needs of the poor.   To
quote Winstanley again: "At this very day," he
wrote in 1650, "poor people are forced to work
for 4d. a day and corn is dear.   And the tithing-
priest stops their mouth and tells them that 'inward
satisfaction of mind' was meant by the declaration,
'The poor shall inherit the earth.'   I tell you the

Scripture is to be really and materially fulfilled . . . You jeer at the name of Leveller. I tell you Jesus Christ is the Head Leveller." [42] Elsewhere this same benevolent mystic warns the rich "Pharaohs" who have "rich clothing and full bellies," their "honours and ease," that "the day of judgment is begun and that it will reach" them ere long. "The poor people you oppress shall be the saviours of the land. If you will find mercy, let Israel go free; break to pieces the bands of property." [43] Some of the Anabaptists set aside the quietistic principles they had learned from their Dutch teachers and reverted to something like the revolutionary program of their German predecessors at Muenster, although the majority remained quiet in their discontent. The Fifth Monarchy men under Harrison are the stormy petrels of revolution, drawing to themselves "many of the most violent and desperate spirits." "Though they speak great words of the reign of saints and seem to invite none but the holy seed," said an official report, "yet the baits they lay to catch men are the taking away customs, excise, taxes, tithes." [44] Even the early Quakers had their radical wing and this group was the one which seemed to the seventeenth century to represent characteristic Quakerism. "It was learnt, that, though they were never seen with a weapon in their hands, several had been found with pistols under their cloaks. A Quaker took up his position at the doors of Parliament and drew his sword on a group of members. When questioned, he replied, that he was inspired by the Holy Spirit to kill every man that sat in the House." [45] But whether by revolutionary activity, or in quiet waiting for the manifestation of the apocalyptic kingdom, or by patient non-resistance, all phases of the movement looked toward social amelioration and sought redress for the wrongs of the poor. With its emotional piety it mated the social radicalism of the gospel and so qualified as a genuine religious movement of the disinherited.

Misunderstood, not so much because of its own excesses as because of the prejudices of those who profited by the existing order—including the clergy —without competent leaders save one, rejected by Cromwell, persecuted and derided, the movement seemed bound to collapse, like that of the Anabaptists in Luther's day. It was saved by George Fox. That typical church of the disinherited which he gathered out of the religiously and economically homeless souls of the day, in which a Winstanley, a Lilburne, a Plockboy, Fifth Monarchy Men, and Anabaptists found refuge, lived because it denied itself the way of violence, overcoming the recklessness of its enemies within. Choosing the way as well as the aim of the gospel it survived the persecution and contempt of Presbyterians, Anglicans and Independents, Republicans and Royalists. It is interesting to note that in the case of the English sects as in that of the German the method of non-resistance was not espoused until efforts toward a violent revolution had been found unavailing in the face of the superior power of the ruling classes, while, at the same time, the ideal of a new social order was abandoned in favor of a sectarian organization of mutual aid and brotherhood. Yet the Quakers, even more than the Anabaptists, continued to represent the social idealism of the churches of the disinherited. Their love of equality, symbolized in the refusal to uncover their heads, and in the use of the familiar "thee" and "thou," their refusal to participate in war, their attitude toward slavery, their production of men like Bellers, whose Christian socialism greatly influenced Robert Owen, their continued support of humanitarian activities, all of these indicate the revolutionary source of the movement and represent an effective continuation of its democratic ethics. But, like the Anabaptists before them, the followers of Fox and Winstanley were prevented from becoming a really inclusive church of the disinherited by the persecutions which isolated them and drove them back upon themselves to form a narrow sect with group loyalty and sectarian consciousness largely taking the place of the larger idealism which inspired the founders. Out of the rejection of the religion of the disinherited a new denomination once more took its rise.[46]

CHAPTER THREE

THE CHURCHES OF THE DISINHERITED
(Continued)

I

The Quakers, no less than their predecessors among the churches of the poor, soon settled down to an "equable respectability." They accommodated themselves to the social situation and confined their efforts toward social reformation to the work of gaining converts to their faith, to the works of charity and to occasional efforts to influence public opinion on social questions. A number of factors were responsible for this decline in revolutionary fervor. The effect of persecution has been pointed out. Another important factor in the development of such denominations from revolutionary groups to settled social bodies, content with their place in the scheme of things, is the substitution of a second generation, which holds its convictions as a heritage, for a first generation which had won these convictions painfully and held them at a bitter cost.[1] But most important among the causes of the decline of revolutionary churches into denominations is the influence of economic success. The churches of the poor all become middle-class churches sooner or later and, with their need, lose much of the idealism which grew out of their necessities. There is no doubt of the truth

[54]

of Max Weber's contention that godliness is conducive to economic success. From the days of Paul at Thessalonica onward, Christianity has not failed to exhort its adherents "that with quietness they work and eat their own bread," while at the same time it has commanded them to abstain from luxury, but, having "food and covering," "therewith to be content." Monastic asceticism, supported by a dualistic view of life, carried the second of these ideas to its extreme, and was rejected by Protestantism, but the Reformers introduced in place of the "extra-worldly" asceticism of the monks an "intra-worldly" asceticism, which regarded work in trade and vocation as the primary duty of life and a service to God; yet they continued to condemn any indulgence in the comforts and luxuries of life as sinful.[2] Restrictions on consumption accompanied by emphasis upon production have their inevitable result in an economic salvation which is far removed from the eternal blessedness sought by the enthusiastic founders of the Protestant sects, but which is not less highly valued by the successful followers of later generations. This process, which is repeated again and again in the history of Christian sects, also took place in the case of the Quakers. In the second and third generations, with the aid of the prosperity prevailing in the days of good Queen Anne, this church of the disinherited became a more or less respectable middle-class church that left the popular movement from which it originated far behind. It continued to hold the tenets of its social program but now as the doctrines of a denomination rather than as the principles of inclusive social reconstruction. In America, especially, the economic rise of the Quakers was speedy and permanent.

Once more, therefore, the poor were without a gospel. The Millenarian hopes which had fired the popular movement of the seventeenth century with enthusiasm were definitely left behind. The ethics of Jesus was dissolved completely into a mild morality of respectability. Eighteenth-century England, ecclesiastical and academic as well as political, feared nothing so much as enthusiasm. Its reaction against the tense emotionalism of Civil War and Revolutionary days, its disillusionments, its lack of vital energies, exhausted as it was by the turbulent passions of religious and political revolt, left it sterile and cold in religion, enamored only with the bleak beauty of mathematically-minded philosophy or, more frequently, indifferent to the claims of any ethical or religious idealism. Lecky, describing the religion of the period, writes, "The sermons of the time were almost always written, and the prevailing taste was cold, polished and fastidious." "As is always the case, the habits prevailing in other spheres at once acted on and were influenced by religion. The selfishness, the corruption, the worship of expediency, the scepticism as to all higher motives that characterized the politicians of the school of Walpole; the heartless cynicism reigning in fashionable life which is so clearly reflected in the letters of Horace Walpole and Chesterfield; the spirit of a brilliant and varied contemporary literature, eminently distinguished for its sobriety of judgment and for its fastidious purity and elegance of expression, but for the most part deficient in depth, in passion, and in imagination, may all be traced in the popular theology. Sobriety and good sense were the qualities most valued in the pulpit, and enthusiasm and extravagance were those which were most dreaded." [3]

Whatever were the contributions which the Enlightenment made to the progress of religion—and that they were important none need doubt—it is evident that the period had nothing to offer the untutored and the poor by way of escape into emotional salvation nor by way of promise of social redemption. "The interval between the accession of Anne, in 1714, and the death of George II, in 1760, is a period in the religious history of England to which neither Churchmen nor Dissenters can look back without shame and regret," writes Fisher. "Puritanism had not only lost a great part of its influence, but also a great part of its vigor. A prevalent indifference and scepticism, the spread of vice, partly a heritage from the last Stuart kings, and the ignorance of the clergy, did not lessen a whit the acrimony of ecclesiastical disputes." [4] Lecky has drawn a vivid picture of the low estate of the clergy. They were largely recruited from the lower economic classes, it is true, and so they might have been in a position to interpret Christianity to the people; but, on the one hand, they were too closely attached to the gentry, from whom they derived their livings, to feel any real concern for the needs of their fellows, while, on the other hand, too many were grossly ignorant of the content of Christianity and without appreciation of its meaning.[5] Bishop Burnet wrote in 1713 of those who came to be ordained that "they can give no account, or at least a very imperfect one, of the contents even of the Gospels, or of the Catechism itself." [6] The "moral and intellectual decrepitude" of the universities, which were "the seed-plots of English divinity," in part reflected, in part brought about the low estate of the clergy.[7]

Such was the religious situation. Social and economic conditions presented a different aspect. England was more prosperous in the first half of the eighteenth century than it had been for many years. But that prosperity, as is usually the case, only tended to accentuate class differences by flaunting in the faces of the poor the luxury which they helped to create but could not share, and by calling forth in the fortunate that sense of superiority which flourishes where possession has no relation to merit. Class distinctions were apparently more real in the days preceding and during the Methodist revival than they had been at any time since the rise of Puritanism. This stratification of society played its part in excluding from the churches of the nobility and the middle class the unwanted and uninterested poor— uninterested in the comfortable, æsthetically pleasant, and morally soft religion of the well-to-do.

During the second half of the eighteenth century,

moreover, this tendency toward stratification in English society was greatly accelerated by the industrial revolution. The old ties which had bound laborer and employer together in the feudal relationships of agriculture or in the patriarchal connection of master and apprentice were broken by the coming of the factory. The wage system and uncertainty of employment, rising capitalism and the competitive order, the growth of the cities and the increase of poverty widened the cleft between the classes. Lecky summarizes the situation by writing that "wealth was immensely increased, but the inequalities of its distribution were aggravated. The contrast between extravagant luxury and abject misery became much more frequent and much more glaring than before. The wealthy employer ceased to live among his people; the quarters of the rich and of the poor became more distant, and every great city soon presented those sharp divisions of classes and districts in which the political observer discovers one of the most dangerous symptoms of revolution." [8]

II

Revolution occurred, as it had always occurred under similar conditions in the past, and again it was a religious revolution, for these disinherited classes furnished the material for the Methodist revival. As a religious movement, it is true, Methodism was not as spontaneous in character as had been the insurgencies which preceded the rise of the Quakers or of the Mennonites; it was much more dependent upon leadership than these had been. But the need was present and the highly trained Oxford Methodists offered the poor a type of faith and religious life which met their needs. While the primary leadership was supplied by the upper classes the secondary leaders, the lay preachers and the membership, with little exception, were derived from the lower economic and cultural orders of society. The people who gathered in the Foundery in London were of the lower economic class with some small sprinkling of the well-to-do. The weavers of Bristol, the miners of Kingswood, the colliers and keelmen of Cornwall and Staffordshire and Wales—these were the groups whence Methodism drew most of its converts. In his "Advice to the People Called Methodists" John Wesley himself points out to his followers that they "have been hitherto, and do still subsist, without power (for you are a low insignificant people), without riches (for you are poor almost to a man, having no more than the plain necessaries of life), and without either any extraordinary gifts of nature, or the advantages of education; most even of your teachers being quite unlearned and (in other things) ignorant men." [9] The opponents of the movement frequently seemed to think it a major argument against its value that it was composed of a "rag-tag mob," of "a set of creatures of the lowest rank, most of them illiterate and of desperate fortunes," while its leaders were called "the heads and spiritual directors of hot-brained cobblers." [10] It is true of course that converts were also gained from other ranks of society.

A description of a Methodist congregation mentions not only numbers of poor people, "thieves, prostitutes, fools, people of every class" but also "several men of distinction, a few of the learned" and merchants.[11] Cowper belonged to the movement himself and testified to the presence of some members of the upper classes of society in the couplet "We boast some rich ones whom the Gospel sways, and one who wears a coronet and prays," [12] referring to Lord Dartmouth. The Countess of Huntingdon's adhesion to the movement was responsible for making it rather fashionable in some circles. But the attitude of the upper classes on the whole was probably truly, if somewhat extravagantly, represented by the Duchess of Buckingham in her letter to Lady Huntingdon: "I thank your ladyship," she wrote, "for the information concerning the Methodist preachers. Their doctrines are most repulsive and tinctured with impertinence and disrespect towards their superiors, in perpetually endeavouring to level all ranks and do away with all distinctions. It is monstrous to be told that you have a heart as sinful as the common wretches that crawl the earth. This is highly offensive and insulting, and I cannot but wonder that your ladyship should relish any sentiments so much at variance with high rank and good breeding." If such honesty was rather singular the attitude was not.[13] It is evident from all sources that persons of wealth and influence were comparatively rare in eighteenth-century Methodism and that when the division between the conventicle and the established church was finally completed it was the group of the disinherited which found its home in the chapel while those whose social position allied them with Anglicanism found it quite possible to maintain their Evangelicalism within the pale of the establishment.

The characteristic features of the new denomination also marked it off as a church of the poor. Its emotionalism made it at the same time an abomination to the enthusiasm-hating upper classes and the salvation of those for whom religion needed to mean much more than prudential counsel and rationalized belief, if it was to mean anything at all. The emotionalism of Methodism, evident in the extravagances of the Bristol revival and in the whole tenor of its preaching and experience, had the same significance as had the demand for direct experience among Anabaptists and Quakers. It was the only way religion could become real to the class which composed the movement; it furnished that group with a psychologically effective escape from the drudgeries of an unromantic, unæsthetic life. "To an ordinarily cultivated mind," as Lecky well states the situation, "there was something extremely repulsive in [the Methodist teacher's] tears and groans and amorous ejaculations, in the coarse anthropomorphic familiarity and the unwavering dogmatism with which he dealt with the most sacred subjects, in the narrowness of his theory of life and his utter insensibility to many of the influences that expand and embellish it, in the mingled credulity and self-confidence with which he imagined that the whole course of nature was altered for his convenience. But the very qualities that impaired his influence in one sphere enhanced it in another. His impassioned prayers and exhortations stirred the hearts of multitudes whom a more decorous teaching had left absolutely callous. The supernatural atmosphere of miracles, judgments and inspirations in which he moved invested the most prosaic life with a halo of romance. The doctrines he taught, the theory of life he enforced, proved themselves capable of arousing in great masses of men an enthusiasm of piety which was hardly surpassed in the first days of Christianity, of eradicating inveterate vice, of fixing and directing impulsive and tempestuous natures that were rapidly hastening towards the abyss." [14] The moral effectiveness of this emotional religion was, of course, its most significant feature. Religious enthusiasm declined in later days because Methodist Christianity became more literate and rational and because, with increasing wealth and culture, other escapes from the monotony and exhaustion of hard labor became available. The substitution of education for conversion, finally, played its part in making revivalism less important for successive generations.

The lay character of the movement, no less than its emotionalism, was also typical of the poor man's Christianity. The use of lay preachers in Methodism, as among Anabaptists and Quakers and in related medieval movements, was due to many factors connected with the economic and social status of the membership: to the unwillingness of a settled and salaried clergy to participate in the popular religious revolt, to the people's antagonism to a professional class which they regarded—sometimes wrongly, sometimes correctly—as being without real understanding of and sympathy with the needs of the disinherited, to the ability of the lay preacher to meet the new group on its own terms, to the simple fervor and naïvely genuine piety of the unsophisticated missionary. A conversation between Robinson, Archbishop of Armagh, and Charles Wesley illustrates several of these points. "I knew your brother well," said the bishop; "I could never credit all I heard respecting him and you; but one thing in your conduct I could never account for, your employing laymen." "My Lord," replied Wesley, "the fault is yours and your brethren's." "How so?" asked Robinson. "Because you hold your peace and the stones cry out." "But I am told," objected the bishop, "that they are unlearned men." "Some are," answered the Methodist, "and so the dumb ass rebukes the prophet." His lordship, as Tyerman adds, said no more.[15]

The ethics of Methodism distinguished it no less from the churches of the middle class and the gentry, although at this point the movement represented a marked departure from the religious revolts of the poor in preceding centuries. It has been maintained with some right that the Methodist movement had the same significance for England that the Revolution had for France. Its democratic character—religious as it was in inspiration and effect—had a marked influence upon the social order. It was responsible for creating a considerable sentiment for greater democracy among many of the wealthier citizens of the nation, whether or not these became adherents of the movement and despite the fact that the majority may have shared the sentiments of the Duchess of Buckingham. It inspired among these an extensive philanthropic activity which resulted in the founding of scores of eleemosynary institutions and in the humanitarian legislation of the early nineteenth century, which was sponsored, in large part, by the Evangelical disciples of Wesley in the Church of England. Among the poor members of the societies it fostered, as all such movements have done, a high degree of mutual aid and co-operation and laid the foundations for popular education. After all Methodism largely represented the religious aspect of that great revolutionary movement of the eighteenth century which placed the individual at the center of things and so profoundly modified all existing institutions.[16]

Despite these influences upon social ethics, however, Methodism was far removed in its moral temper from the churches of the disinherited in the sixteenth and seventeenth century. Briefly, the difference lay in the substitution of individual ethics and philanthropism for social ethics and millenarianism. It has been pointed out that the distinctive ethical note of the churches of the poor in the earlier periods was due to the interest of the constituency in salvation from social evils, from class inferiorities, injustices, and oppressions and that these movements derived much of their driving force and enthusiasm from the millennial hope. A second characteristic of their ethics, the emphasis upon humility, frugality, and democracy, was partly religious in origin, partly due to a natural tendency to exalt the typical virtues of the poor, supported as these virtues are by the teaching of Jesus. With respect to the first point, the ethical approach of Methodism was apparently quite different from that of Anabaptism or seventeenth-century millenarianism. It had some interest in the economic fortunes of its constituency and in the social inequalities from which they suffered, but it was much more interested in the correction of their vices, from the point of view of their religious fortunes. The ethics which it had in mind was not the social ethics of the Sermon on the Mount but the sober, individual ethics of "The Serious Call" and of Moravian piety. It was in one sense of the word much more of a religious and less of an ethical movement than were its predecessors. The religious interest preceded the social and social idealism remained more or less incidental, while the hope of a thoroughgoing social reconstruction was almost entirely absent. Indeed, it may be maintained that the socially beneficial results of Methodism were never designed, but that they accrued as mere by-products of the movement.

This difference in temper between the earlier churches of the poor and Methodism doubtless had much to do with the latter's success in a class-governed world, which feared nothing so much as social revolution and easily defeated the enthusiastic millenarianism of previous movements. Despite the mob-violences from which Wesley and other Methodist preachers suffered in the early years of the revival, persecution in their case was not comparable with that meted out to Baptists and seventeenth-century democrats. Methodism was never subject to the same official oppressions and grew respectable in a much briefer time than these required.

The difference in ethics was due to a number of causes but primarily, it seems, to the fact that the Methodist movement remained throughout its history in the control of men who had been born and bred in the middle class and who were impressed not so much by the social evils from which the poor suffered as by the vices to which they had succumbed. The character of a religious movement is probably more decisively determined by its definition of the sin from which salvation is to be sought than by its view of that saving process itself. The primary question to be asked for the understanding of a Fox, a Paul, a Luther, a Wesley as well as of Old Testament prophets and of the founders of non-Christian religions, such as Buddha, Zoroaster, Mohammed, is this: what did they mean by sin or evil? from what did they want to save men? Now it is evident in Wesley's case that he envisaged sin as individual vice and laxity, not as greed, oppression, or social maladjustment. Sin meant sensuality rather than selfishness to him and from Wesley the entire Methodist movement took its ethical character. Wesley was more offended by blasphemous use of the name of God than by a blasphemous use of His creatures.

He was much more concerned about swearing in soldiers' camps than about the ethical problem of war and the useless sacrifice of soldiers' lives or the righteousness of their cause. "My soul has been pained day by day," he wrote to the mayor of Newcastle, "even in walking the streets of Newcastle, at the senseless, shameless wickedness, the ignorant profaneness, of the poor men to whom our lives are entrusted. The continual cursing and swearing, the wanton blasphemy of the soldiers in general, must needs be a torture to the sober ear, whether of a Christian or of an honest infidel. Can any that either fear God or love their neighbor hear this without concern? especially if they consider the interest of our country, as well as of these unhappy men themselves. For can it be expected that God should be on their side who are daily affronting Him to His face? And if God be not on their side, how little will either their number, or courage, or strength avail?" [17] Apparently Wesley believed that the justice of a cause was quite secondary in the eyes of God to the personal purity of its defenders. In the rules for the band societies the same conception of sin meets us: their members are to abstain from evil, especially from buying or selling on the Sabbath, tasting spirituous liquors, pawning, backbiting, wearing needless ornaments such as rings, ear-rings, necklaces, lace, and ruffles, and taking snuff or tobacco.[18] It is not to be denied that Wesley achieved an eminent success in delivering the poor from many of their worst vices by the one-sided emphasis upon sin in its

[68]

individual aspects, and it may be that the vices of eighteenth-century English colliers and soldiers stood in such high relief that social evils appeared insignificant beside them; yet one must remember that the usual picture drawn of the brutalization of the working classes of the time was largely inspired by the Evangelical view of the situation. In the much greater moral problems involved in the new social relationships brought about by the industrial revolution or present in the age-old relations of the classes Wesley and Methodism had no real interest.

Even in so far as social interests and influences were present Methodism betrayed the bias of its middle-class leadership. The reform movements were supported largely by the Evangelical party in the church of England and did not represent the efforts of the poor to help themselves. Wilberforce and Hannah More, Kingsley and the Christian socialists set forth the social spirit of the movement; there were no leaders of the people of the type of Winstanley or Harrison.[19] The social ethics of Methodism was an ethics of philanthropy and humanitarianism, which regarded movements toward equality as concessions made out of love rather than as demands of justice, and this philanthropy suffered the constant danger of degenerating into sentimental charity. But the typical social ethics of the poor is an ethics of reconstruction whose excrescences appear in violence rather than in sentimentality. Thus Methodism was adapted from its beginnings to become a church of the respectable middle class, even though the emotionalism of its religion continued to make a strong appeal to the untutored.

Other factors, beside this original middle-class point of view in Methodism, were responsible for its early rise into a higher economic and cultural stratum. Wesley himself faultlessly described the process whereby other churches of the disinherited, and his own with them, sloughed off their original character. "Wherever riches have increased," he wrote, "the essence of religion has decreased in the same proportion. Therefore I do not see how it is possible in the nature of things for any revival of religion to continue long. For religion must necessarily produce both industry and frugality, and these cannot but produce riches. But as riches increase so will pride, anger, and love of the world in all its branches. How then is it possible that Methodism, that is, a religion of the heart, though it flourishes now as a green bay tree, should continue in this state? For the Methodists in every place grow diligent and frugal; consequently they increase in goods. Hence they proportionately increase in pride, in anger, in the desire of the flesh, the desire of the eyes and the pride of life. So, although the form of religion remains, the spirit is swiftly vanishing away. Is there no way to prevent this—this continual decay of pure religion? We ought not to prevent people from being diligent and frugal; we must exhort all Christians to gain all they can, and to save all they can; that is in effect to grow rich. What way then can we take, that our money may not sink us into the nethermost hell? There is one way and there is no other under heaven. If those who gain all they can, and save all they can, will likewise give all they can, then the more they gain, the more they will grow in grace, and the more treasures they will lay up in heaven." [20] It is quite significant that Wesley omits all reference to the manner in which Christians are to gain all they can. But the passage well describes the rise of Methodism in the Old World and later in the New from a church of the poor to a middle-class church, which, with its new outlook, abandoned the approach to religion which made it an effective agency of salvation to the lower classes in the century of its founding. In England this development was not dissimilar to that of the Quakers, and Methodism remained somewhat sectarian in character, but in America the result, for reasons which will become apparent, was the growth of a church in the true sense of the word which attracted to itself the most substantial classes of the citizenry. In both cases, however, the economic and cultural character of the movement underwent profound modification and, sooner than was the case with the other movements, this religion of the disinherited became a respectable church of respected classes. Originally urban in character it retained the loyalty of the tradesmen and workers who, rising in the social scale through their thrift and diligence, became the small and later often the great capitalists of the growing cities of the nineteenth century. More than Presbyterianism or Congregationalism Methodism came to be the re-

ligion of business classes. Methodism left behind the
emotionalism of its earlier years and adapted its
ethics, never typically lower-class in character, to
the needs of its rising clientele. It abandoned lay
preaching in favor of a regular and theologically
trained ministry; it modified and softened in many
ways the original stringency of its methods; it gave
up its old program of mutual aid, so typical a feature
of the religion of the poor; it left aside the semi-
ascetic character of its early communities and ar-
ranged its rules to accommodate those whose interests made the world-fleeing ethics even less practicable than it was for the poor.[21] Once more a religious revolt, issuing in the formation of a sect, led
finally to the establishment of a middle-class church,
a yielding servant of the social order.

III

The Methodist revival was the last great religious
revolution of the disinherited in Christendom. And
it was not wholly a popular movement. Perhaps
that is one reason why it was the last. It is a striking fact that the revolutionary tendencies of the poor
in the nineteenth century were almost completely
secular in character, while in preceding eras they
were always largely religious in nature. The socialism of 1848 and later years was closely akin in many
ways to Anabaptism and Quakerism as well as to
Lollardy and the Waldensian revolt. It cherished
as these did the hope of an inevitable social renewal
which would cast down the mighty from their seats

and exalt them of low degree. Like these it provided the oppressed with an emotional escape from the weariness and grime of uneventful and profitless labor. Like these it brought to consciousness the latent sense of social solidarity and endowed the impoverished individual life with the significance of participation in a cosmic event. But for the angels who fought on the side of Baptists and Quakers it substituted economic laws, and in place of the early coming of the Son of Man it anticipated the class struggle and the dictatorship of the proletariat. What were the reasons for this change?

The conditions which preceded the rise of socialism were not dissimilar to those which formed the background of the religious revolutions of previous centuries. There was present the actual exclusion of the poor from churches grown emotionally too cold, ethically too neutral, intellectually too sober, socially too aristocratic to attract the men who suffered under the oppression of monotonous toil, of insufficient livelihood and the sense of social inferiority. There was present also the awakening of the disinherited to the consciousness of their human dignity and worth. But the result was not a religious revolt. On the contrary socialism often assumed the character of an anti-religious movement. Its secularism was doubtless due to many causes—to the growth of the scientific temper and of nineteenth-century materialism, to the prevalence of the mechanistic conception of life which industrialism fosters, to the determinism of the Hegelian philosophy in which Marx had been

trained, to the bare fact that the leaders of the movement were not religious men. But among the causes
of this secularism the absence of an effective social
idealism within any of the Christian churches was of
especial importance. The last previous religious
movements among the disinherited, Methodism and
Pietism, had failed to follow in the steps of the Baptists and Quakers. They had allowed the millenarian hopes to lapse; they had substituted for the
concept of the kingdom the symbol of heaven; they
had been concerned with the redemption of men from
the hell beyond the grave alone and had held out little
promise of salvation from the various mundane hells
in which the poor suffer for other sins besides their
own. So they had failed to keep alive within the
church those realistic hopes which had always been
the source of new religious uprisings in the centuries before; and they had joined with the older
churches in proclaiming a purely other-worldly hope.
In any other century of Christian history this failure
to keep alive the promise of social amelioration
through Christian ethics and by divine miracle might
have had less far-reaching results. In the century
of inventions and of industrial production, in a time
so largely occupied with the present world and its
values, the absence of this social element from the
preaching of the gospel was fatal to the religion of
the disinherited. It is significant that much of the
leadership of the social movement now came from a
group which had been nurtured in the ideals of Old
Testament prophecy, and which even when it lost

its religious faith did not fail to give expression to ideals which had been derived from that religion. The leadership of the Jews in the social revolutions of the nineteenth and twentieth centuries had these religious sources; it was the only effective substitute for the Christian leadership which had once been unfailingly available in every crusade for justice but which had died out, perhaps as a result of attrition in a theological and other-worldly church.

The nineteenth century, it is true, did not entirely lack representatives of the naïve religious movements. The Salvation Army is an outstanding example of the manner in which a separate conventicle must be formed by the religious poor, who have been excluded from the denominations of their newly enriched brothers. But Booth was neither a Francis nor a Wesley. The movement he inaugurated was not a popular movement of spontaneous character; the very organization of the Army implied a home-mission enterprise rather than a religious and social awakening. Moreover the under-privileged of the modern era have been too greatly alienated from the gospel as well as from Christianity, whether by the silent forces of the industrial environment, or by the strident voices of Marxian apostles, or by the indifferent attitude of churchmen, for the Army to be able to repeat the successes of its victorious predecessors. Other contemporary movements of the religious poor toward the attainment of adequate religious experience and expression come to light in many a gospel tabernacle and evangelistic society and millenarian association. But the mass of the workers remains untouched; there is no effective religious movement among the disinherited today; as a result they are simply outside the pale of organized Christianity. Yet without the spontaneous movement from below, all efforts to repristinate the ethical enthusiasm of the early church and to reawaken the Messianic hope are unavailing. The churches which again and again have been recalled to consider a neglected message by the religious revolutions of the unfortunate are so much the poorer because there is no sect of the disinherited today. Even sectarianism is preferable to the absence of vital Christian conviction and expression among those whose hunger and thirst after righteousness is not any the less necessary to the world because it has natural roots.

CHAPTER FOUR

THE CHURCHES OF THE MIDDLE CLASS

The frequent association of Christianity with the social revolutions of the poor, as well as its original emphasis upon the virtues of the meek, have led various theorists to make the generalization that the faith is essentially proletarian in character. Most famous of the definitions of Christianity from this point of view is Nietzsche's dictum that it is the religion of slaves. But interpretations of an opposite sort, which have sought to explain Christianity in terms of middle-class or bourgeoisie psychology have not been wanting. Anti-Christian socialists have constantly sought to identify the church with the bourgeoisie and to demand the destruction of the institution along with the elimination of the class. So eminent a social scientist as Max Weber has lent some support to this judgment, which ascribes to the whole of Christianity the evident characteristic of much of modern Protestantism. Just as the nature of Confucianism was determined by its relations to the official and literary class of China, he writes—as the character of orthodox Vedantic Hinduism was due to Brahmin leadership, as the quality of Buddhism was the consequence of monastic supremacy and the content and temper of Islam the result of the dominance of the Arabian military class, so "Christianity, during all the periods of its internal and external development, in ancient times as well as in the Medieval Age and in Puritanism, was and remained a specifically urban, above all, bourgeois religion." [1]

Such an interpretation of Christianity may be nearer the truth than is the popular assumption of its essentially rural character or the Nietzschean definition; yet it also remains a sweeping generalization which does scant justice to the appeal the gospel has had for all sorts and conditions of men or to the relations of the church in history to aristocracy on the one hand and proletariat on the other. It is the universalization in theory of a temporal and partial situation—of the modern alliance of capitalism and Protestantism. Yet Weber's statement directs attention to the fact that some periods of Christian history were strongly influenced by the interests of the middle class and that many modern denominations had their source as separate organizations in these interests rather than in the common needs of humanity.

It is necessary here, as in the case of the churches of the poor, to qualify the theory of class denominationalism by reference to the rôle of prophetic leadership. The heroes of the bourgeois churches, from whom these derived much of their doctrine and piety, often transcended class and economic conditions to set forth a purely religious ideal with divine disregard for mundane interests in caste or in financial security. Yet the acceptance of their ideals by a particular group, and the modification of the religious doctrine by selective emphasis has often been due to other than purely religious motives. Sombart's fundamental dictum holds good: "Think as you like of the genius of the founder of a religion, this much is clear—that before any religion can strike root certain conditions must exist. Economic conditions are of the number, but they are not the only ones. Biological and ethnological factors play a very important part too. . . . This disposition in a people [for some religion] will be influenced more and more by economic conditions the nearer we approach our own times, seeing that economic life, anyhow in the modern history of Western Europe, has dominated man to a greater and greater degree." [2] The interaction of these various factors—the religion of the prophetic leader, economic, biological, ethnological and political conditions—is as evident in the case of the bourgeois churches as in the case of national and proletarian denominations. But though this interaction may obscure, it does not hide, the dominantly middle-class character of many modern Protestant churches. One of the most enlightening contributions made to church history by sociology and economics is the revelation of the connection between capitalism and Calvinism as set forth by Cunningham, Weber, Tawney, and their followers. Despite the overstatements which have marked the rise of the theory connected with these names, it is not possible to disagree with the fundamental contention that a close relation has existed in modern times between these two great social movements and that they have profoundly influenced each other. The conservative conclusion which may be drawn for the purposes of our study from the evidence amassed is that the Calvinistic denominations in general are representative middle-class churches, whose rise and development as religious groups were conditioned by the economic interests of the bourgeoisie and the economic rise of whose members as a middle and capitalist trade class was strongly influenced by the faith of Geneva.

I

The religious needs of the middle class are not as well defined as are those of the poor, for the bourgeoisie present a more complex pattern both of sociological structure and of social interests than do the proletarians. Political and cultural interests combine with economic desires in various ways, while the relationship of the governing class—the bureaucracy—and of the professional class with the group engaged in trade is often very close and subjects the latter to many modifying influences. Furthermore, the development of individual self-consciousness, with the resultant love of personal liberties and rights, is responsible for considerable variation in the religion as well as in the politics of the bourgeoisie. Yet the psychology of the middle class contains certain constant features which are reflected in its religious organizations and doctrines. Among these the most important are the high development of individual self-consciousness and the prevalence of an

[80]

activist attitude toward life. To these primary factors others of secondary importance may be added: the general level of education and culture in the group, the financial security and physical comfort which it enjoys, the sense of class which it fosters, and the direct effect of business and trade upon its code of ethics.

The individuals of no other group, save those of the professional class, are so highly self-conscious as are the members of the bourgeoisie. Various elements in their situation are responsible for this fact. The character of their employment which places responsibility for success or failure almost entirely upon their own shoulders is fundamental. In contrast to the worker, who, in ancient as in modern times, is accustomed by his co-operative labor to share or to resign responsibility and to cultivate a sense of dependence for success upon impersonal factors, the business man is employed in relatively independent activity, in which he must rely upon his own energy and acumen. His dealings, while not so purely personal in character as are those of professional men, still remain dealings with men as buyers and sellers even more than dealings with goods to be bought and sold. Moreover, the level of education is relatively high in the middle class and contributes a share to the development of a sense of self. Finally, the rise of the bourgeoisie in the face of the feudal powers was conditioned by the development of the doctrines of natural rights and individual liberty and the ideals forged in that conflict have been conserved in the literature and tradition of the commercial groups. In consequence the men of the middle class think in terms of persons more than of forces, and in terms of personal merit and demerit more than of fortune and fate.

Hence the religion of these groups is likely to be rather intensely personal in character. The problem of personal salvation is far more urgent for them than is the problem of social redemption. In middle-class symbolism conceptions of heaven in which individual felicity is guaranteed are much more important than the millennial hope of the poor man's faith—a difference, which, of course, is also partly due to the greater satisfaction of the middle class with the temporal order in which it enjoys a considerable number of pleasant advantages. The dominance of self-consciousness is further responsible for the preoccupation of much bourgeois religion with the problem of evil and with the task of justifying the ways of God to man. Where self-consciousness is highly developed the sensitiveness of the individual is correspondingly great, the need for solace in a world "so careless of the single life" is pronounced, and religion is required to exercise the office of the comforter with exceptional attention and skill. Where the sense of solidarity is greater, as on the whole it is among the poor, a far greater readiness prevails to accept without explanation and without rebellion the common fate of pain and loss and death. The attitude of resignation which the disinherited have imbibed with mother's milk is the difficult achievement of the middle-class man. In harmony with this whole emphasis upon the fate, the salvation, the happiness, the worth of the individual in bourgeois faith, there is a corresponding emphasis upon the personal character of God. The impersonal conceptions of mysticism are quite foreign and unintelligible to this group.

The corollary of the emphasis on self-hood is the activist attitude toward life which prevails in the middle class. The very existence of the class depends on the technical manipulation of things and the management of persons. Life is not regarded as a time of enjoyment and contemplation but as the sphere of labor. Business is the very essence of existence and industry the method of all attainment. This "practical rationalism" characterizes not only the middle-class conduct of economic enterprise but also its conceptions of ethics, politics, and religion. The values of religion are regarded less as a divine, free gift than as the end of striving; the method of religion is held to be the method of constant activity; the conception of God is the conception of dynamic will; the content of the faith is a task rather than a promise. "Active asceticism—not the possession of God or contemplative surrender to the Divine which are regarded as the highest good in the religions influenced by aristocratic and intellectual classes—but activity willed by God and carried on with the sense of being God's tool, could become the preferred religious attitude among the bourgeoisie," says Weber, who finds in this dynamic view of religion and in this practical rationalism in the conduct of life the distinguishing mark of bourgeois faith.[3] This attitude in religion is reflected not only in the conceptions of God and of the content of his will but also in the doctrines of personal responsibility, of the priesthood of all believers and in the ideas of sin and of salvation. The conception of God which prevails in bourgeois faith is that of dynamic will. God is neither the Absolute of the mystic nor the Father of the child-like meek; He is rather the Old Testament Jehovah of energetic activity and of stern legislation, the Creator and the Judge more than the Redeemer and the Savior. The attempt has often been made to correlate the doctrine of predestination, which prevailed in the Calvinist middle-class churches, with the character of the Puritan, but it is difficult to conceive either that the doctrine was the outcome of bourgeois psychology, with all its emphasis on individual responsibility, or that, conversely, the Puritan character of dynamic activity was the result of the doctrine of predestination. There is truth in the statement that Calvin, in the doctrine of predestination, "did for the bourgeoisie of the sixteenth century what Marx did for the proletariat of the nineteenth" by giving "assurance that the forces of the universe are on the side of the elect"; [4] but, on the whole, this element derived by Calvin from purely religious sources was hard to reconcile with the native interests of the bourgeois mind and suffered an early eclipse wherever the trading class was dominant. Only in so far as the idea of God as dynamic force and sovereign will came to expression in the doctrine of predestination was the latter thoroughly germane to the temper of the middle classes.

The ideas of sin, righteousness, and salvation which flourish in the middle-class milieu are profoundly influenced both by this dynamic conception of life and by the sense of individual worth and responsibility. Sin is not so much a state of soul as a deed or a characteristic; it is not so much the evil with which the whole social life and structure is infected as it is the personal failure of the individual. That interpretation of moral evil which mystic and ascetic achieve and which finds sin in the very essence of mundane and human existence is foreign to the middle-class point of view. The pluralistic rather than the monistic conception of sin prevails; sin is not so much status as act. Similarly, righteousness is a matter of right actions carried out in obedience to a series of divine commandments. It is very necessary, therefore, that religion establish a code of right conduct; a general spirit of well-doing is insufficient or irrelevant. Such righteousness, moreover, is an individual matter. Though the righteousness of society be the aim, yet it is the righteousness of a society of discreet selves, who one by one obey the divine precepts under divine and human compulsion; it is, in short, the righteousness that is by law, not by faith. The doctrine of salvation falls into line with these conceptions of sin and of the good life. Salvation is conceived as a process within the indi-

vidual, not the construction of a divine kingdom; its
results are believed to be given to the individual in
conversion or in a process of education which establish him as a holy character, distinguished not so
much by heroic as by conforming virtue. He is delivered not from sin and guilt, from remoteness from
God, from the sense of the utter worthlessness of all
human effort, but from bad habits and evil desires
which war against the divine command.

The religious ethics of the middle class is a
product of the same interests modifying the tradition
or the moral deliverances of the religious leader. As
in the case of the poor, the sanction of religion is
invoked upon the peculiar virtues of the group itself;
honesty, industry, sobriety, thrift, and prudence,
on which the economic structure of business as well as
the economic and social status of the individual depend, receive high veneration while the virtues of
solidarity, sympathy, and fraternity are correspondingly ignored.[5] A very high regard attaches to
the ethics of family life; this emphasis is partly due
to the special appreciation of the family that prevails in a class which finds its social satisfactions
almost limited to this group and which, moreover, can
nurture a high type of family life under the prevailing conditions of individual freedom and responsibility. On the other hand this interest in family
morals may also be due to the threat to stable family
relations which arises out of this same individualism.
It may be, too, that the emphasis on family is a
natural concession which an individualistic tradition

makes to the suppressed social character of religion; interest in this institution is made to do service for the neglected social factors in faith.

The religious ethics of the middle class is marked throughout by this characteristic of individualism. The good which is to be sought in ethical life as in religion is the moral welfare of the individual. Because his economic life has taught him always to weigh cost and price against each other and because it has demonstrated the relationship of personal ability and energy to success, the man of business is inclined to construct his whole view of the providential order on the Deuteronomic pattern. Success in the world is to him a clear evidence of the presence of virtue and failure an almost certain symptom of vice. "Convinced that character is all and circumstances nothing, he sees in the poverty of those who fall by the way, not a misfortune to be pitied and relieved, but a moral failing to be condemned, and in riches, not an object of suspicion—though like other gifts they may be abused—but the blessing which rewards the triumph of energy and will." [6] Such an ethics is capable of producing a real heroism of self-discipline and, in its insistence on personal responsibility, the courage of resistance to the authority of state and church when these conflict with the imperatives of individual conscience. But this morality is incapable of developing a hopeful passion for social justice. Its martyrs die for liberty not for fraternity and equality; its saints are patrons of individual enterprise in religion, politics, and economics, not the great benefactors of mankind or the heralds of brotherhood.

Finally, the organization of the churches of the middle class, like their doctrine and ethics, reflects the individualism and the activism which rise out of the economic life. These churches are typically democratic in constitution, designed to give free scope to the individual, yet to preserve morality, to train character, and to fulfil in their very structure the demands of the divine will. Hence the churches of the bourgeoisie tend to accept some type of representative government which will insure liberty and individual responsibility but which will also raise barriers against the license of complete democracy. Their constitutions contain not only a doctrine but also a discipline and their leaders are not only teachers but also guardians. The leader is democratically chosen; he has none of the special unction of the priest, and yet he may assume high authority as the interpreter and executive officer of the divine will. It is significant, however, that in the churches of the middle class this type of organization is justified not by its fitness for the end which it serves but by its conformity to the will of God as expressed in the Scriptures. Others may appeal to expediency, the bourgeois seeks here as elsewhere to observe the letter of the law that he may in no manner violate the sacred principle of contract.

Middle-class religion, so defined, is not only distinguished from the faith of the poor but also from the Christianity of the landed gentry and their allies or dependents. For the latter type is agricultural or military, while bourgeois religion is commercial and industrial in symbolism and attitude. The one kind of organization is paternal and institutional, the other democratic; the best ethics of the one class is the ethics of *noblesse oblige*, that of the other the morality of strict self-discipline without much regard for the neighbor; the doctrine of the one centers in a magic conception of salvation and of the means of grace, that of the other in the teaching of salvation in and by character. Hence the religion of the bourgeoisie seeks separate organization not only on account of the economic conflicts of the class with aristocracy above and the proletariat below but also because of the divergent religious attitudes and desires which arise out of these class differences.

II

Upon the whole the acquisition of a bourgeois type of religious faith is not an heroic achievement, accomplished by dramatic revolt from prevailing conceptions, but rather the product of a slow process of accommodation to the developing interests and experiences of a rising economic group. The development of Methodism and, in part, of Congregationalism, illustrates the manner in which a church of the poor sloughs off its original endowment and accepts a type of religious life more in conformity with its new economic interests and status. Yet there have been periods in religious history when the interests of the bourgeoisie have asserted themselves so powerfully as to assist materially in the founding of new churches in revolt against those organizations of Christianity which ignored their specific desires and needs. Such churches were founded in France, the Netherlands, and Switzerland in the sixteenth century and in England in the seventeenth century. More recently a middle-class church of a type quite distinct from that of the earlier groups came into being in the United States under the leadership of Mary Baker Eddy.

In the Catholic church of the later Middle Ages the religion of the poor was represented—imperfectly, it is true—by the friars and mystics. The religious and political interests of the nobility were provided for by the institutional and autocratic character of the Roman organization and by the considerable freedom from papal suzerainty enjoyed by various groups of the aristocracy; there was room for dissatisfaction here, of course, as the development of the German Reformation showed. The long connection of medieval Catholicism with the social order in which peasants, craftsmen, and nobility formed the chief classes had brought about a mutual accommodation; the church on the one hand and the social classes on the other were phases of one common stable culture. It was the newly rising middle class, connected with the expanding commerce of the later medieval time, which found itself least at home in a social order based on agriculture and military enterprise and in a church whose attitudes and forms had been established in an entirely different cultural milieu. The restrictive social ethics of Catholicism with its persistent tendency to regard economic life from the point of view of consumption rather than of production, with its suspicion of all economic enterprise as worldly employment, with its prohibition of interest and its effort to establish fixed prices, weighed upon these new classes heavily despite the practical disregard of the canon laws and their continued modification, from the time of Thomas Aquinas onward. Furthermore, the Catholic conception of the good life as supremely represented in monastic asceticism with its poverty and remoteness from all economic activity and the Catholic view of religion as essentially the contemplation of the love of God were anything but sympathetic to the active, wealth-seeking spirit of the new bourgeoisie.[7] Again, the church was the religious guardian of that feudal order with which the new capitalism found itself in frequent conflict. Hence in order that it might establish itself in the social order it was necessary for the new middle class to discover and to secure the adoption of a new social philosophy in which individual ability and the value of economic enterprise would be recognized no less than hereditary privilege and the value of political or military leadership. Finally, the great wealth of the church, a wealth which was often poorly administered from the moral as well as from the economic point of view, aroused the antagonism of a class which was struggling to acquire what others possessed without effort.

When Luther gave the signal for revolt against the medieval church the disaffected of all sorts of men rallied to his banner. There were among the

Protestants those whose interest was purely religious and who revolted against the secularization of the church; there were among them the peasants and the proletarians who were weary of specious promises and sought the immediate realization of their long nurtured hopes; present also were the humanists in rebellion against the irrationalism of superstitious customs and beliefs, and the knights whose national or provincial interests had been threatened by the Holy Roman Empire and the imperial church; and there were among the Protestants, finally, the enterprising bourgeoisie, fired by past successes and the promise of the future, seeking to establish themselves and their interests in spite of restraints laid upon them by aristocracy and hierarchy. But when the disturbances of the early years had passed it was discovered that humanism and the religion of the disinherited either had deserted or had been excluded from the new movement and that in one section the Reformation had been captured by the middle class while in another section the nobility was in control. Calvinism prevailed in the former area, Lutheranism in the latter. The Reformation was not, to be sure, a "revolt of the rich against the poor" but in its final outcome it established churches which offered religious sanctuary to bourgeoisie and nobility but sent the poor away empty to find some other home for their faith.

Most of the Calvinist churches at that time acquired and have since retained a definitely middle-class character. It is noteworthy that the geograph-

ical distribution of this form of Protestantism co-
incided very early with the geographical location of
the rising commercial classes. Swiss cities on the
trade routes between northern and southern Europe,
the commercial cities of France, the provinces bor-
dering on that main artery of commerce—the Rhine,
the Netherlands, which at the time were the center of
banking and commerce, England, in which Puritanism and the new capitalism arrived together a hundred years later, finally America—these were the
scenes where commercialism and Calvinism both
triumphed. Venice and Florence, earlier centers of
trade, also were sympathetic to the new faith and but
for the victory of the feudal houses over the commercial interests might have welcomed the Reformation. Scotland forms a notable exception to this
geographical coincidence of commercialism and
Calvinism; in the absence of a bourgeoisie it was the
nobility which adhered to the Reformation in this
country as in Germany. Yet in the course of time
the association of commercialism and Calvinism also
became established among the Scotch. This peculiar
relationship of bourgeoisie classes to Calvinism is
marked even by their coincidence in smaller areas
than nations or in social classes within mixed religious
populations.[8]

The geographical distribution of Calvinism is not
the only significant clue to its character as a middle-
class church. While it is true that in its early days
it appealed to all sorts and conditions of men, at-
tracting by the purity of its doctrine and the warmth

of its piety the sincerely religious souls of all classes yet it is also evident that in the course of time it repelled the poor—in Switzerland, the Netherlands, and England—causing them to form their own sects, and that it was unable to invade, except in greatly diluted form, the Reformed churches of the aristocracy, such as the Church of England and the state churches of Germany. In the course of time the middle-class character of the Calvinist denominations became more and more pronounced and today they find their members, in England, in America, in the Netherlands, primarily among the classes connected with trade and the control of industry.

The origin of the association between the new faith and the new commercial classes may have been more or less due to those irrational, merely given, factors, which play so large a rôle in history—to the appearance of Calvin in Switzerland, to the accidents of language and race, to the ease of communication between commercial centers and the consequent dissemination of religion from one to the other. But the continuation of that association throughout the centuries must be due to more rational causes. In part it is to be explained by the correspondence existing between the principles of the Reformed faith and the religious and moral interests of the bourgeoisie, in part by the ability of Calvinism to produce a middle class through its insistence on those virtues which made the growth of trade and industry and so of the bourgeoisie possible, in part by the success of the economic group in modifying the religion to meet its desires.[9]

With regard to the first point, primary importance attaches to the harmony of the Calvinist conception of individual rights and responsibilities with the interests of the middle class. There has been a plain relationship in history between the religious, the economic, and the political doctrines of individual liberty. England, said Montesquieu, excels in piety, commerce, and liberty. *Laissez faire* and the spirit of political liberalism have flourished most in the countries where the influence of Calvinism was greatest, in Switzerland, Holland, England, and America. In the second place, the dynamic conception of life emphasized by the new faith was highly compatible with the spirit produced by the new economic activity. The God whom Calvin proclaimed was the energetic Lord of creative and providential will, not the object of reposeful contemplation; and despite the doctrine of predestination the new faith demanded a corresponding activity on the part of men. Not the *visio dei* but the doing of His will was the characteristic of the religious life. Righteous conduct could not, indeed, merit heaven, but such conduct was regarded as the inevitable result of divine grace. "Since conduct and action," as Tawney writes, "though availing nothing to attain the free gift of salvation, are a proof that the gift has been accorded, what is rejected as a means is resumed as a consequence, and the Puritan flings himself into practical activities with the demonic energy of one, who, all doubts allayed, is conscious that he is a sealed and chosen vessel." [10] While Calvinism probably was not responsible for the development of this activist attitude, it was highly agreeable to men who were accustomed strenuously to seek their material welfare and who had learned that diligence in this field is far better repaid than unanxious reliance upon the provident processes which give harvests to idle birds and beauty to lilies. Again, the new faith was compatible with the interests of the commercial classes in its interpretation of the kind of conduct demanded by God. For one thing it gave religious sanction to the enterprise of business man and industrialist by regarding it as a divine calling, not inferior but superior to that ascetic life which Catholicism had glorified and which, implicitly as well as explicitly, had fostered among Christians a low estimate of trade as a worldly and spiritually vulgar employment. Moreover, Calvin and his followers adapted the strict social ethics of Catholicism to the situation of urban and trade classes especially in such matters as those of interest and banking, where they relaxed, grudgingly but effectively, the laws against usury. Finally, Calvin's appeal to the Old Testament ethics was singularly fitted to support the bourgeois' self-esteem and sense of position by teaching him what he was very ready to believe—that prosperity is the reward of virtue and poverty the affliction of sin. Thus the Calvinist could build his social ethics on the foundation first used by that other great entrepreneur, the Jew; both were free from the inconvenient counsel of Jesus on wealth and the devotion to mammon.[11] In these and other ways the painful dichotomy between the world and Christianity, between business and religion, was overcome. "In the Calvinist ethics there was created for the second time (after the Thomistic ethics) a great unified conception, which enabled the Christian to be active in the world with a good conscience and without a break between the Christian-ethical and the worldly ideals." [12]

Because Calvinism stood for these conceptions of the Christian life it not only was agreeable to the commercial classes but contributed not a little to their increase and success. Max Weber's well-known thesis to the effect that Calvinism was one of the major sources of modern capitalism is probably too great a simplification of the actual process. After all, capitalism preceded Calvinism and has flourished apart from this type of Christianity. Rationalism and humanism were not without important influence on the development of the modern capitalist system. Yet there is some truth in the statement that among the complex processes which brought forth the economic structure of the western world the Genevan faith takes an important place. By its insistence that Christians show forth the fruits of salvation in energetic activity, by its sanction of economic enterprise as divine calling, by its praise of an intraworldly asceticism which was diligent in production and frugal in consumption, by its nurture of an individualistic temper which became capable of revolting against the authority of the state as well as of the hierarchy, Calvinism did much to foster the

growth of the middle commercial classes of Switzerland, Holland, England, and America.[13]

Yet the agreement between the interests of the
middle classes and the religious temper of the Reformation movement was not so complete but that
the former should not find in the doctrine of the
God-intoxicated French reformer inconvenient elements which they felt impelled to modify. However
close the relationships between economics and theology may have been in the sixteenth century and however practical may have been the genius of Calvin,
he was after all, like Augustine and Luther and Wesley, a prophetic personality in whom the religious
interest was quite supreme; to it he ruthlessly subordinated all other values which less radically Christian men continued to hold dear. The Genevan
discipline illustrates the point. The complete dominance of the church over the political and economic
life of the city was the fundamental assumption of
Calvin's theocratic régime as it was in the repristi-
nated Calvinism of New England a century later.
The preachers of Geneva continued to fear money as
the root of all evil and surrounded its acquisition with
many prohibitions supported by threats of everlast-
ing punishment. Despite their insistence on individual responsibility, their distrust of human nature
was so profound and their theocratic ideal so compelling that they sacrificed liberty to authority without a qualm.[14] "Calvinism had little pity for poverty," says Tawney, "but it distrusted wealth, as it
distrusted all influences that distract the aim or relax

the fibers of the soul, and, in the first flush of its youthful austerity, it did its best to make life unbearable for the rich." [15]   But this position was not long tenable before the assaults of the class which had found the doctrine otherwise so attractive and to which the church needed to look for its chief support.

It may well be that the failure of the restrictive ethics was due to an antinomy within the soul of Calvinism itself—to the clash of the dynamic individualism fostered by its religious teaching with the repressive character of its morality.   Individualism triumphed, however, only after the commercially and politically interested groups within the church threw their influence into the scale—quite unconsciously— and conveniently forgot the discipline while they remembered the liberty their faith inculcated. [16]   The modification of primitive Calvinism under this influence is marked in four particular areas: in the democratization of the originally autocratic and authoritative plan of government, in the abandonment of the essentially medieval social ethics, in the substitution of independency and tolerance for the conception of the church-state, and in the acceptance of doctrinal modifications under the influence of the humanism and rationalism which were prevalent in the middle classes. [17]

Calvin's distrust of the common man and his aristocratic temper, as well as his doctrine of the divine sovereignty, inclined him toward an essentially autocratic plan of church government.   Both in Geneva and in early New England the theocratic ideal was associated with oligarchical rather than with democratic polity. Yet Calvinism has everywhere entered into close alliance with democratic movements in both church and state. While the origin of such tendencies was usually humanist or radical rather than religious, yet the Reformed faith was predisposed to their acceptance partly by its insistence on individual responsibility and the priesthood of believers, partly by the influence of republican Geneva on the ideas and habits of its youth, and partly by the convenience of the liberal doctrine in the conflicts of Protestants with Catholic monarchs in France, the Netherlands, Scotland, and England.[18] Under the further influence of the commercial classes who became the leaders of the democratic revolts of the sixteenth and seventeenth century in order that they might be delivered from royal monopolies and restrictions on commerce Calvinism took on an increasingly republican character. Yet the same middle class which sought in religion the sanction of its efforts to achieve liberty from royal control found in that very faith a convenient reason for denying the same liberty to the poor and the ungodly. The doctrine of predestination and the practice of government by the righteous and respectable few were corollaries in Switzerland, Holland, and New England. Not until the genuinely democratic ideals issuing out of humanism and the revolts of the poor had come into decided conflict with the oligarchical principles of Calvinism did these countries achieve really democratic constitutions.[19] Nevertheless, the individualism of the commercial class broadened the popular basis of the Calvinist church and state, far removed as they were from any desire to recognize the principle of universal equality.

The second modification of primitive Calvinism which resulted from its alliance with the middle class was the relaxation of its restrictive social ethics. Calvin was little inclined to abandon the medieval principle of the supremacy of the church over all other institutions and of religion over all other interests of life. Indeed the ecclesiastical regulation of economic life was far more rigorously enforced at Geneva by the new than it had been by the old church. But under the subtle influence of the business interests which the church had welcomed into its fold the restrictive regulation soon lost its force, while the commendation of the commercial life as a sphere of divine vocation and the religious invigoration of individual activity remained effective. So, in discipline more than in doctrine, there was substituted for the collective authority of the church the equally orthodox authority of individual conscience. While the church continued to be regarded as the rightful arbiter of family morals and even of political conduct, its official representatives were persuaded of the self-sufficiency of economic ethics. So the Calvinism which "had begun by being the very soul of authoritarian regimentation," "ended by being the vehicle of an almost Utilitarian individualism." [20]

Finally, Calvinism was modified so as to assume a more definitely middle-class character through the influence of humanism and rationalism, and nineteenth-century science. The middle classes developed their interest in the liberal movements of thought because of the education which their economic circumstances enabled them to afford, because of the close relationship existing between rationalism and the social philosophy of modern business enterprise and, in later times, because of the technical interest which industry and commerce were required to take in the development of modern science. It has been pointed out by critics of Weber's thesis of the Calvinist parentage of capitalism that such typical representatives of the bourgeois spirit as Franklin and Carnegie derived their social ethics from the Illumination rather than from the Reformation.[21] Yet the middle classes in general received this new influence quite unconsciously, unaware of any antagonism between the rationalism they absorbed in education and business and the teachings of their churches. Moreover their increasing affluence inspired them with ever greater self-respect—the reflection of the esteem, it may be, in which they were held by other groups. The desire to achieve a demonstrable success, regarded as a token of election, the ethics of merit and reward in the mundane life, the activism and individualism of Calvinist religious attitudes combined with rationalist appreciations of progress in the conquest of nature and of the value of the human reason to liberalize the strict teachings of early Calvinism. The supreme doctrine of the sole sovereignty of God lost its significance as the rather considerable sovereignty of man over nature came to light and as his imperial instincts were aroused in the competition of economic life. Under such influences Grotius and Locke were eventually alienated from the Calvinist system of thought and such movements as Arminianism and Unitarianism broke away from the parent stem. In them the related doctrines of human ability and of limited divine sovereignty were combined with the teaching of self-help and with faith in human progress. But even where the modification of the original doctrine did not go to such lengths as in these instances, the slow deterioration of the early Calvinist doctrines was nevertheless noticeable, though its explicit expression was held in check by the confessionalism fastened on the church in the sixteenth century. In the one case the victory of middle-class psychology over the religious spirit of Calvin came patently to light, in the other cases it was no less present though it was obscured. In New England Congregationalism, in Dutch Calvinism, and in English and Scotch Presbyterianism, as well as in Unitarianism and Arminianism, the accommodation of the doctrine and attitude of the erstwhile strictly theocentric faith to the spirit of the middle class resulted in the blunting of the sharp edges of the doctrine of divine sovereignty and in a practical emphasis on salvation by character. The ultimate result of this victory of middle-class attitudes over Calvinism was the substitution for the spiritual exaltation of the early devotees of a decent morality which believed with Defoe that "with energy, ingenuity and resolution it is possible under the most unfavorable conditions to make this life more than tolerable and even to arrange one's future affairs on a satisfactory footing with an offended Deity." [22] What a far cry this is from the pilgrim's heroic progress toward the celestial city! No better description of this decline of Calvinism is possible than Dowden's much quoted paragraph: "After the jagged precipices and forlorn valleys— scenes of spiritual exaltation and despair—a table-land was reached—safe, if unheroic—where men might plow and build. To make the best of both worlds was the part of prudence, and of the two worlds that on which our feet are planted is, at least, the nearer and the more submissive to our control. Divine providence is doubtless to be acknowledged, but it is highly desirable to supplement Divine providence by self-help." [23]

The victory of the bourgeoisie over Calvinism, however, was to be made even more complete than appeared in later English Puritanism. It remained for America to carry the accommodation of the faith to bourgeois psychology to its extremes. A single line of development leads from Jonathan Edwards and his great system of God-centered faith through the Arminianism of the Evangelical revival, the Unitarianism of Channing and Parker, and the humanism of transcendental philosophy, to the man-centered, this-worldly, lift-yourself-by-your-own-boot-straps doctrine of New Thought and Christian Science.[24] The common strand that runs through these various movements is the adaptation of the early faith to the changing attitudes of the bourgeoisie.

In its final phase the development of this religious movement exhibits the complete enervation of the once virile faith through the influence of that part of the middle class which had grown soft in the luxury the earlier heroic discipline made possible by its vigorous and manly asceticism. Here the gospel of self-help has excluded all remnants of that belief in fatality which formed the foundation of Puritan heroism. Here the comfortable circumstances of an established economic class have simplified out of existence the problem of evil and have made possible the substitution for the mysterious will of the Sovereign of life and death and sin and salvation, the sweet benevolence of a Father-Mother God or the vague goodness of the All. Here the concern for self has been secularized to its last degree; the conflicts of sick souls have been replaced by the struggles of sick minds and bodies; the Puritan passion for perfection has become a seeking after the kingdom of health and mental peace and its comforts. This is not the religion of that middle class which struggled with kings and popes in the defense of its economic and religious liberties but the religion of a bourgeoisie whose conflicts are over and which has passed into the quiet waters of assured income and established social standing. Yet it remains the religion of a middle class which excludes from its worship, by the character of its appeal, the religious poor as well as those who live within the lower ranges of economic and cultural respectability.

CHAPTER FIVE

NATIONALISM AND THE CHURCHES

Among the social forces which contribute to the formation of classes and so to the schism of churches, economic factors may be the most powerful; but they are not the only sources of denominationalism. Sometimes, indeed, they seem to be less important than ethnic and political or generally cultural factors. Alongside of the churches of the poor and of the bourgeoisie, ethnic and national churches take their place as further manifestations of the victory of divisive social consciousness over the Christian ideal of unity.

The extent to which the church of Christ has failed to overcome, even in its own structure, the political divisions of men and has allowed itself to become compromised by them is obviously revealed on the continent of many nationalities, Europe, and in the nation of many races, the United States. When European critics point a scornful finger at the multitudinous sects of the New World and ascribe their presence to "the typically American" spirit of individualism, they ignore the rather patent contribution which the "typically European" spirit of nationalism has made to this variety of religious experience and organization. A realistic analysis of the American religious scene shows that its variegated pattern has been drawn to a large extent by European immigrants who have made the United States the crucible of many churches as well as the melting-pot of many races.

A bare list of the Christian denominations in America indicates the importance of ethnic and national factors in dividing the church. Among the names one notes in such a list are: German Seventh Day Baptists, German Baptist Dunkards and Scandinavian Independent Baptists; Albanian, Bulgarian, Greek, Rumanian, Russian, Serbian, and Syrian Orthodox Churches; the Armenian Apostolic and the Assyrian Jacobite Churches; the Reformed Church of Soviet Russia, and the Polish National Catholic Church; the Norwegian Lutheran, the United Danish Evangelical Lutheran, the Danish Evangelical Lutheran, the Finnish Evangelical Lutheran National, and the Swedish Evangelical Free Churches; the Eielsen, Icelandic, Suomi, Slovak, and Norwegian Lutheran Synods; the Swedish Evangelical Mission Covenant, the Norwegian-Danish Evangelical Free Church Association, the Moravian Church, and the Evangelical Union of Bohemian and Moravian Brethren. All of these exhibit racial character in their names, but there are many other churches which have dropped their nationalist or ethnic titles without losing their racial character or which have never expressed in their names their otherwise obvious racial complexion. Among these are the Old Catholic Church in America (Lithuanian and Polish), the

Amana Society (German), The Evangelical Church (German), the Evangelical Synod of North America (German), the United Lutheran Church, the Joint Synod of Ohio, the Iowa Synod, the Lutheran Synod of Buffalo and the Jehovah Conference (all German), the Augustana Synod (Swedish), the Lutheran Free Church (Norwegian), the Apostolic Lutheran Church (Finnish), the Evangelical Lutheran Synodical Conference (German) and various German Mennonite groups. To these should be added the churches of an even earlier European immigration. The Presbyterians are as Scotch or Scotch-Irish in character as the Lutherans are German or Scandinavian; the Protestant Episcopal Church is still an English church, the two Reformed Churches are Dutch and German, the United Brethren are German in origin. The list of immigrant denominations can be continued and might include eventually the Congregationalist and Baptist churches which are also, though indirectly, a part of America's inheritance from the European union of national culture and religion.[1]

Nationalism, the influence of which on denominationalism becomes apparent in this American potpourri of churches, is not a simple phenomenon. Among its various significant aspects the ethnic, the cultural and the political need especially to be distinguished. The first of these is occasionally regarded as primarily responsible for the divisions of the religious as well as of the political life of Europe. Thus it may be maintained that Catholicism is primarily the religion of the Mediterranean and Alpine ethnic stocks and that Protestantism is the faith of the Nordics. Catholicism, it will be pointed out, flourishes in the south of Europe, in Italy and Spain. It finds adherents, also, among those more northern populations whose Teutonic character has been attenuated by the infiltration of much Alpine blood, as is supposed to be the case in southern Germany. Protestantism seems to show a strange affinity for the blue-eyed and fair-haired races of the north-Germans, Scandinavians, and Anglo-Saxons. Even the Huguenots of La Rochelle were Nordics, it is claimed. From this point of view religious differences ultimately derive from differences in the biological characters of the races. Simple and attractive as such a solution of the problem of religious differentiation may appear, it is obviously not true as a complete theory. Nordic Catholics, such as the Irish (who are sometimes assumed to be Alpines or Mediterraneans for the purposes of the theory) and Mediterranean Protestants, such as the Welsh, and mixed races, such as the Protestant Swiss and the Catholic Bavarians, offer more exceptions than can be easily fitted into the rule. A modicum of truth may attach to the argument for the ethnic basis of religious differentiation, but the social attitudes and customs of behavior and thought which are the foundation of religious organization are transmitted less through physical heredity than through the institutions of civilization. A member of the Alpine race is likely to be a Catholic, it is true; but it cannot be proved that the germ plasm from which he took his rise contained tendencies toward individual subordination and reliance upon institutions. It is far more reasonable to suppose that the historical connection of Catholicism with the culture and the social institutions of his environment provided him with an early training which made Catholicism seem to him to be the most rational and acceptable faith. The Catholicism of Mediterranean countries, as well as of Ireland, is rooted not so much in the ethnic character of the peoples as in historical conditions, which, however influenced by ethnic factors, have been subject also to other and more decisive influences. Ethnic heredity alone is insufficient to explain the nature of any aspect of a culture—its politics, its art, its economic life, or its philosophy; the religion which is intimately interwoven with these other contents of the social mind can scarcely be explained by reference to that factor alone. Perhaps religion is as often responsible for ethnic character as the latter is responsible for the faith; so in the case of the Jews and of the Armenians, and today in the case of south European Catholics in America, religion is a very important factor in the preservation of racial character.[2]

The cultural quality of nationalism, therefore, rather than its ethnic character must be considered as one of the probable sources of denominationalism. Denominations, like the nations of which they are originally a part, are separated and kept distinct by differences of language and of habitual modes of thought rather than by physical traits and the former are often only incidentally rooted in the latter.

In conjunction with cultural influences political factors must be considered in their bearing on the division of Christendom. We are prompted to note their importance in effecting schism by a score of events in church history from the days of Constantine to the Russian Revolution and the recent reorganization of Balkan politics and religious life.

I

When the Christianity of the first three centuries entered into alliance with the Roman empire to become the religion of the world-state, its leaders could scarcely have been aware of the extent to which they were surrendering the supra-national ideals of Jesus and Paul. For it was a denationalized and universal empire with which they associated the ecumenical ambitions of their faith, and it was a relatively catholic culture which they were called upon to infiltrate with their pan-human ethics. In its religious and cultural cosmopolitanism this civilization was as far removed as any culture could be from that nationalistic and separatistic spirit which Judaism represented and which had furnished the apostle Paul with the occasion for developing the universalistic interpretation of the gospel. Though the early sectarian idea of Christianity, represented by its conception of itself as a kingdom of God opposed to the kingdom of the world, continued to be maintained as an undertone in the whole movement toward the identification of church and state, yet Christian leaders could regard the Cæsar as a divine representative, the political head of a new theocracy.[3]

As soon as this close relation between the church and the state was consummated, however, the continuance of a universal church was predicated on the continuance of a universal empire and the establishment or maintenance of a universal culture. For not only would the state's interest in the church and the church's interest in the state be certain henceforth to bring ecclesiastical schism in the wake of political separations but the accommodation of Christianity to the prevalent culture, which the position of a privileged church made inevitable, was bound to involve the church in every disintegration of cultural unity. From this time onward the ethics and, in part, the doctrine of Christianity came decreasingly to be the presentation of the teachings of Jesus and increasingly the religious formulation of prevailing social ideals. And this formulation could not escape the fate of whatever culture it represented and sanctioned. At the beginning of the fifth century the chief visible result of the triumph of Christianity, says Guignebert, was that it was a triumph in appearance only. "Far from having transformed the Græco-Roman world, Christianity was really absorbed by it and applied to its own atavistic needs and customs in the whole domain of both mind and body." So the church became "one of the different aspects of the Roman state," which, "with its machinery and its gifts of administration, its insistence upon order and regularity" had also "taken over its dread of too original and overenthusiastic individuals, who agitate and confuse the simple minded, and interrupt the lilt of long-hallowed social rhythm." [4] Under such circumstances it was inevitable that the secularized church should share the fate of the secularized culture.

Political and cultural disintegration came to the Roman empire and with it the disintegration of the great church. The social history of the long controversies between Arian, Nestorian, Monophysite, and Orthodox Christians and all the resultant sectarian movements is still largely obscure. There is probable truth in the statement that "the struggle against Arianism was not merely a struggle for orthodoxy," but that "Athanasius was really at the head of a national Greek party resisting the domination of a Latin speaking court," so that "from this time onwards Greek patriotism and Greek orthodoxy" became almost convertible terms.[5] Certainly the historians are right who contend that the Nestorian and Monophysite churches, the St. Thomas Christians, the Armenians, the Syrian Jacobites, the Coptic and the Abyssinian churches, were not primarily heretical sects distinguished from the great Eastern church by theological heterodoxy, but conservative national churches which protested against the innovations of the see of Constantinople.[6] These earliest schismatic movements in the church apparently had their social sources in the conflicts of provincial groups with the empire. But the first great schism of the church, which divided East and West, was clearly due to political and cultural rather than to religious and theological motives. Theological disputes about the addition to the creed of the innocent word *"filioque"* or about the use of unleavened bread at the Eucharist were symptoms of a deeper cleft between the East and the West than theological uniformity or ecclesiastical unity could heal. The age-old cultural differences between Hellenic East and Roman West, the division of the empire, the barbarization of the one section by invading Nordics and of the other by migrating Slavs, the political ambitions of the bishops at Rome and Constantinople, these are the more authentic sources of the schism.[7] The designation of the two churches, which resulted from this division, as the Greek and Latin churches is a much more apt definition of their essential differences than is a theological explanation of creedal variations between them. Language is always the carrier of culture and the terms Greek and Latin represent the contrasting cultural character of the two sections of ancient Christianity. The differences which are connoted by these terms were, of course, reinforced by divergences in the types of the new peoples who entered upon the heritage of the Greeks in one instance and of the Romans in the other—Slavs in the East, Teutons in the West. Yet it was the Latin spirit with its practical interest and genius for organization which determined the most important characteristics of the one church and it was the conservation of the Græco-Christian theology and ritual which gave the other its typical individuality.[8]

The ensuing history of these two branches of

Christianity reveals even more clearly than the schism does how political and cultural factors influence the development of denominations. Since the days of Constantine the Eastern church had frankly recognized the spiritual as well as the temporal overlordship of the emperor. Closely attached to the political organization as it was, it could not but disintegrate as the Byzantine power declined and made way for rising Slavic nationalities. To this day it remains a unified church only in so far as its various sections represent the common religious aspects of that common, Eastern, Byzantine-Slavic culture which the church itself largely transmitted to the new peoples of Russia and the Balkans. But in so far as its organization is concerned, it is simply a congeries of national churches, for it has acquiesced in every division of its establishment made desirable by the shifting forces of political interest.[9] At least nine independent national churches are recognized in consequence of this principle. One by one the churches of Cyprus, Mt. Sinai, Greece, Serbia, Rumania, Montenegro, of the old Austrian-Hungarian empire, of Russia and Bulgaria, separated themselves more or less completely from the four patriarchates of the ancient church, while the latter were divided from each other when Turkish conquest deprived them of the unifying influences of a common culture and a common political overlordship. The division of the Eastern church is greater than even this formidable list of thirteen separate organizations indicates, for the church in the old Austrian empire consisted of four virtually independent sections, divided by racial lines, and the exarchate of Georgia pursued a separate course from the church of Russia. The political reorganization of the Balkans after the war of 1914-18 naturally brought the reorganization of the politically divided churches in its train. Out of the Serbian, the Karlowitz Serbian, Dalmatian and Cattaran, the Bosnian and Herzegovinan and the Montenegrin churches, a single church of Yugo-Slavia is seeking to organize itself, not without facing the same difficulty in reconciling ancient racial and cultural differences as that with which the new political state must contend. A similar situation prevails in the new Rumanian church which represents the reorganization of the churches of Rumania, Transylvania, Bukowina, and Bessarabia. "The greatest hindrance to the reorganization of the Orthodox church in the Balkans and in Rumania," a recent authority states, "is the exaggerated national feeling and jealousy of each country against the others. This jealousy is much more felt between the different branches of Orthodoxy than between them and the Roman Catholics or Lutherans." [10] So in disintegration and in reintegration the Eastern churches follow the fortunes of political life. Nationalism has not completely triumphed over the Eastern church, for amid all the differences of organization a unity of spirit prevails. Orthodoxy transcends schism. "No such detached, independent churches as we see here belonging to the Orthodox communion would be possible under the papacy," writes Adeney. "Rome is most fearful of schism,

Constantinople of heresy" and the many racial quarrels and partisan differences "do not break the bonds of the deep-seated union of the Holy Orthodox church." [11]   Yet a common orthodoxy does not insure a common ethics; the sphere of the Holy Orthodox church is the scene of many of the bitterest quarrels between professedly Christian nations that the modern world has witnessed.   Orthodoxy no less than heterodoxy has been thoroughly nationalized in this domain of the Christian faith.

II

While Eastern Christianity suffered division as a result of political disintegration but maintained a kind of unity between its divided members because of their common Græco-Slavic culture, the Western church achieved unity for a time by assuming political control of the various nationalities in its area and by becoming the source of their culture as well as of their religion.   The decline of the empire in the West and the development of new nations from the sixth to the eighth centuries led, it is true, to the practical independence from Rome of the Merowingian, West-Gothic, and Anglo-Saxon churches.[12] Had it not been for the return of a Cæsar in the person of Charlemagne, the re-establishment of a united Roman Catholicism would scarcely have been possible.   But with the decline of Carolingian rule and the rise of German nationalism in its stead the unity of the Western church was again threatened.   Now it was the strategy of a new Cæsar, Gregory VII, who was no less an emperor because he was a pope, virtually to combine in the curia the political powers of a Holy Roman empire with the ecclesiastical authority of the Holy Roman Church. It seemed to be evident to him that the existence of the one depended on the existence of the other. His primary problem was that of bringing the German church into effective subordination to the universal church, but that end could be achieved only at the expense of German nationalism itself.[13]

The disintegrating effect of rising Western nationalism next came to light in the conflict of the papacy with the French monarchy. The ambitious power of Philip the Fair could not suffer so great a rival within his own domain as that of the Roman church. Two solutions of the conflict offered themselves. The first one was in line with the expansive and imperial tendencies of the new kingdom; it was the subordination of papal power to the throne of Philip. This was achieved for a time in the "Babylonian captivity" of the church, when the papal seat was removed to Avignon and papal policies were directed by French interests. But the conflict of these interests with those of Italy and Germany, and of England and Flanders, forced the acceptance of another solution of the problem—the division of the church in the great schism which placed rival popes on the thrones of Avignon and Rome for the space of forty years.

The healing of this division did not put a stop to the efforts of the French monarchy, of Parlement, the Sorbonne, and the ecclesiastical princes, to secure the independence of the national church from Rome. The struggle between national and Catholic interests continued down to modern times—to the separation of church and state in 1905—although the Concordat of 1516 virtually separated the Gallican church into an independent establishment subject to the king rather than to the pope and so, in the eyes of the rulers, made the Reformation unnecessary in France.

In England, next of the states to rise to nationhood, the organization of a national church, practically independent of the papacy, took place as early as the fourteenth century. The third great monarchy of the period, Spain, followed in the same path when Ferdinand and Isabella secured the power of exercising the decisive influence on the appointment of princes of the Spanish church. In Naples a similar movement took place. Yet in only one instance did this early tendency toward schism on nationalist lines result in so complete a break as to give rise to a new denomination. This happened in Bohemia under the leadership of Hus, and the denomination which resulted was the Czech national church of the so-called Utraquists.[14] Nationalism in this early period was a political and not yet a cultural principle; the common Latin culture of which the church was the exponent, the common ritual and the common theology were stronger bonds of unity than governmental diversity could readily break. Truly independent churches, capable of quarreling with each other not only about the privileges of appointing bishops and of selling livings but also about the conduct of worship and the niceties of doctrine, could scarcely rise before nationalism had become culturally as well as politically divisive. The independent churches of the pre-Reformation period were merely state churches; national churches began to flourish when the new ethnic cultures were born in the Renaissance and in the economic revolution of the late Middle Ages.[15]

The culture of the medieval world had been a unity. Latin had been its common tongue. Its sense of beauty had been nurtured by a common art which had achieved its highest glory in the cathedrals of France, England, Germany, and Italy. It had shared a common literature, science, and philosophy —the deposit of the ancient world. In feudalism it had possessed a common social organization which had inculcated in the youth of every land the same social attitudes, the same reverential obedience to authority. And all this world looked to the selfsame goal; it was not divided by the partisan hopes of chosen peoples for national glory, but it was united by the common vision of a golden Jerusalem into which men might enter only as citizens of heaven. Science and education—such as they were—were quite as international as in modern times and if the agricultural and guild economic organization of the day did not bring the peoples of Europe into close touch with each other neither did it divide them by competition for markets. There was diversity within this unity, to be sure, but it was not the diversity of conflicting cultures. Kings and knights might fight with each other but their soldiers were mercenaries and the passions of war were aroused in the whole populace only by the common enemy of all Western Christendom—the Saracen. Within this unified culture which it had built and still maintained a catholic church could flourish whatever its conflicts with princes and sectaries.[16]

Nationalism as a principle of culture came to birth with humanism. The Renaissance had its universal aspects but in its practical effects it promoted the diversification of culture. Latin gave way in the mouths of savants and preachers to the once barbarous native tongues. National literature brought national self-consciousness, for language more than anything else is the medium of culture without which the latter cannot grow. Language, however, imposes its limitations on civilization; it is not only a means of communication but often a barrier to wider community. Other movements besides humanism contributed to the rise of national cultures; most important among these was the growing money power which was not only desirous of breaking the shackles of medieval social ethics but also required stable and favorable local governments so that it might pursue its ends without disturbance.[17]

The coincidence of the Reformation with this rise of nationalism may not indicate an intrinsic relation. As a religious movement the reform of the church with its theology and worship might well have taken place without compromise with nationalist ambitions and policies. But, given the political constitution of Catholicism, given the provincial views and petty aims of the Italian papacy of the time, given the political organization of Europe in the Holy Roman Empire, given, also, the reformers' lack of ability to visualize any church save a politically supported one, and given a nationalism which regarded the church's wealth and power with greedy eyes, the outcome could scarcely have been other than it was—the development of divided national churches. Whether the Reformation was taken into tow by nationalism, whether it was driven into the arms of the princes by imperial and papal policy, or whether it was itself responsible for the creation of nationalism—the result was that close alliance between the rising nation-states and the new religious spirit, which became the source of the greatest process of ecclesiastical disintegration in the whole history of Christianity. The Reformation might claim that it was returning to the faith of the first century; but in its organization it relied more on Constantine than on the New Testament church and in its social ideals it came eventually to approximate pre-Christian, particularist Judaism more nearly than Pauline catholicism.

Everywhere Protestant Christianity, consciously or unconsciously, adopted the principles of nationalism and identified itself with a particularist culture. German, Swedish, Danish, and Norwegian Lutheranism, Scotch Presbyterianism, English Episcopalianism, Swiss and Dutch Calvinism accepted the

Roman idea of a church co-extensive with the state, but, defining the state in nationalist terms and rejecting the hierarchy, they subordinated religion to politics and accepted in place of papal sovereignty the rule of a divinely appointed king or of a political parliament chosen by that new voice of God—popular opinion.[18] The history of this disintegration of the new Christianity under the influence of the old and new politics is too well known to require elaborate description. Lutheranism, conservative in temper and frightened by the excesses of the peasants' revolt, sought the protection of territorial princes and free cities. Under their auspices the German Reformation lost much of its popular and spontaneous character; it became a reformation dictated from above rather than a movement arising out of the masses. In the conflicts of French and Hapsburg policies it became still more involved in the politics of the German princes and when, after Luther's death, the Schmalkaldic War broke out, to be followed in the next century by the Thirty Years' War, its subservience to the interests of state became almost complete. Since that day the spirit of Lutheranism has been "the spirit of an isolated national ecclesiasticism." [19] Even in modern times, despite the increasing secularization of the state, this section of the Reformation church has remained the most isolated, most nationalist, and least cosmopolitan of all the Western branches of Christendom. The story of the political origin and guidance of the English Reformation and the consequent nationalist character of the Anglican church is one of the best known chapters in ecclesiastical history. The Calvinist churches of the Netherlands, Switzerland, and Scotland were much more popular in origin and character than the German and English establishments; they represented the Calvinist ideal of theocracy under church auspices, and were greatly influenced by the liberal spirit of the bourgeoisie. Though intimate relation to the state was not lacking, the cultural rather than the political character of nationalism divided these very similar churches from each other. Nevertheless the constitution of these religious organizations as state-churches involved them also in all the quarrels of the nations and distinguished them in their internal character from the free sects. So nationalism did not fail to exercise its divisive effect even upon these later products of the Reformation, for they also found it impossible to resist the sway of the nationalist cultural forces or of a nationalist patriotism which invokes the aid of a racial Jehovah in every crisis of the state and which piously assents to the political doctrine of a chosen people, elected by God to impose its civilization along with its religion on the remaining tribes of the earth.

III

The character of the churches which arose out of the Reformation under these auspices was and remains determined by several principles of organization which distinguish them from other sorts of denominations and which are also the basis for differentiation among themselves. First, in distinction from the sects of the poor, these national churches share with Catholicism, sometimes more, sometimes less, the institutional principle of social organization.[20] Lutheranism, Anglicanism, Presbyterianism, and the Reformed denominations all belong in this category along with the Catholic churches of the East and West. In their conception of the sacraments, of conversion and education and of the office of the ministry they represent the institutional and authoritarian as opposed to the individualistic and democratic conception of Christianity. Differences on these points are to be found among these churches, of course, as the famous controversies between Lutheranism and Calvinism, and between Presbyterianism and Episcopalianism show; but such differences do not obscure the underlying unity of the common conception of the church as an institution rather than as a voluntary society, of the sacraments as means of grace rather than as symbols of confession, of the creeds as standards of doctrine rather than as confessions of faith. This institutionalism is closely connected with the whole conception of the church as a part of the state, or as co-ordinate with the state. The authoritarian conception of the state, which persists even in democracy, may have been originally derived from religion, but in later Protestantism the relationship has been reversed and the church has accepted the attitude of the state with which it was so closely identified.

The second principle which distinguishes the national churches is a corollary of the first. These churches are doctrinal and liturgical in character, regarding conformity to creed and ritual as the essential requirements of Christianity. The sect centers, as a rule, in devotion to a Christian ethics radically different from the social ethics of its contemporary society; the church, which seeks to include within itself the whole cultural group of the nation, leaves the moot sphere of social ethics to the administration of the state, trusts the individual to govern his conduct by his creed, and seeks uniformity primarily within the sphere of belief and worship, where it is least likely to become involved in conflict with the political and economic interests of the nation and its classes. Yet it is not primarily for the sake of expediency that the church emphasizes the doctrinal character of Christianity and tends to neglect its ethical discipline; its whole character as a teaching institution and as a transmitter of grace and salvation makes this emphasis inevitable. Perhaps another reason for the continuation of the doctrinal character of the church is the effectiveness of the whole conception in maintaining control over untheological masses, who can be persuaded that their soul's salvation depends upon assent to true doctrines and that the definition of these must be left to the theological experts. Furthermore, creeds have been the result of statecraft almost as much as of theology. From the Nicene symbol, formulated at the instance of Constantine, to the Westminster Confession, which was framed by an assembly of divines who had been selected, appointed and maintained by the Long Parliament and which was promulgated on the authority of English and Scotch Parliaments, the major creeds of Christendom have been born of the union of church and state. Frequently it has been the state's interest in uniformity which has dictated the formulation and acceptance of a creed by the church. Sometimes ecclesiastical interest in gaining the goodwill of the sovereign was the inspiring motive in creed-making as in the case of the French and Belgic confessions. The non-political sects, on the other hand, have never been greatly interested in formulating theology into standards of doctrine; their slightly developed theological interest has been satisfied by the acceptance of amended editions of the church creeds while their attention has been given to ethics.

The connection of church and state, furthermore, has often influenced the character of the confessions themselves. The Augsburg Confession, presented to the Imperial Diet at Augsburg by the Protestant princes of Germany, was less Lutheran than Luther's theology not only because it was framed by the irenic Melanchthon but also because the princes were interested in the preservation of their ancient rights within the Catholic empire as much as in religious principles and in ecclesiastical independence from Rome. Hence it minimized the differences between Lutherans and Catholics while it exaggerated the contrasts between the former and the Zwinglians and Anabaptists. So the character of the Lutheran church, down to its representatives in twentieth-century America, has remained influenced by the political hopes and fears of German princes in 1530.[21] The thirty-nine articles of the Church of England also reflect the influence of political expediency. The forty-two articles of Edward VI "were thrust on the Church of England in a rather disreputable way." Although they purported to represent the agreement of the bishops and Convocation "they were never presented to Convocation, and were issued on the authority of the king alone." Their Protestantism had its sources not only in religion but also in the greed of the Lord Protector and his associates who coveted the rich estates of the church. Revised under Elizabeth and reduced to thirty-nine, the articles were not published until they had been "diligently read and sifted" by the queen, who, indeed, suppressed the final article for a time in order that England might share the favor which Lutheranism but not Calvinism enjoyed in the Holy Roman Empire.[22] Knox's Scotch Confession was revised by Maitland of Lethington and Lord James Stewart, who "dyd mytigate the austeritie of maynie wordes" and advised the omission of an article which dealt with the "disobediens that subjects owe unto their magistrates." [23] So the devious ways of political intrigue have left their mark on the churches by enshrining in confessions sanctioned for centuries the counsels of political expediency.

National churches, in distinction from the sects, are liturgical in form of worship. In this instance also the ideal of uniformity and the fear of the abnormal characterize the state church as they do the state. The sect seeks individual religious experience and expression, and it frequently designs its technique of worship to call forth the individual phenomena of conversion and inspiration. The church, on the other hand, is content to stimulate a milder, steadier, and more uniform type of emotional life and to represent a less individual, more common human need before the Divine Majesty, in its prescribed forms of worship.

The third characteristic of the national churches is their tendency to restrict the application of Christian ethics to the more individual phases of human conduct or to social conduct within the bounds of the family. The source of this characteristic is, in part, the relation of the church to the state. There are significant differences on this point between Lutheran and Calvinist national churches, but there is also a broad agreement between them and Catholicism in the common acceptance of the state as divinely ordained and of the ethics of the state as relatively divine. The latter is regarded as corresponding to the ethics of nature which is again identified with Old Testament ethics and with the divine regulations for a world of sin. The sect may challenge the authority of the state, but the church as an accommodation group must accept it and fit it into its ethical and doctrinal scheme. It may do this by maintaining that the state holds its power in fief to the church, or by claiming for political authority immediate derivation from God, as in Lutheranism and Anglicanism, or by regarding political authority as divinely derived through the people, as is the case in some Calvinist conceptions. The scheme varies with different circumstances; the Catholic idea of church and state grew out of the political conditions of the earlier Middle Ages; the Lutheran and Anglican conception reflects the relation of the church to princes friendly to the Reformation, the Calvinist idea, which at times approximates the Catholic, had its origin in the conflicts of the Reformation party with unfriendly rulers and in the support of a friendly populace. Hence in Lutheranism and Anglicanism, those types of Protestantism which were most dependent for their success on the rulers, the recognition of the divine right of kings was most explicit and in the countries holding to these faiths kingship has endured longest. The motto which serves as the text of most sermons in times of political crisis in these nations would seem to be: "Let every soul be in subjection to the higher powers; for there is no power but of God; and the powers that be are ordained of God." [24]

The influence of nationalism is further reflected in the attitude of the churches of the Reformation toward other problems of social ethics. Sects may and do condemn war; the nationalist churches must regard it as a part of that relatively divine order of nature which has been instituted in a world of sin; hence they continue to accept war's catastrophes as divine judgments and its successes as divine blessings. Sects may condemn the oath and refuse to participate in government; the churches have been mainstays of the courts of law by enforcing the non-legal sanctions of the oath and they have been the supporters of stable government by teaching that both civil and military service may be divine vocations. Their attitude toward social customs is in general that of acceptance. They are not prone to seek reforms; they are most often the bulwark of political conservatism. Hence they seek to influence the processes of government less than the sects in times of innovation and more than do the latter in times of conservative reaction. This conservative attitude is fortified by a theology and an ethics which draw a clear distinction between the realms of grace and sin, regard the social order as belonging to the latter realm, restrict the ethics of Jesus to the former and so enable the good churchman to live with a relatively easy conscience amid the evils of slavery, the oppressions and privileges of class-governed societies, the exploitation of backward races and the shambles of war. God is conceived here in the likeness of the king; whatever of evil there is, exists somehow by his permission; the good subject will receive in patient resignation whatever life brings of good or ill and will not presume to believe that he may help in any save a passive way to enforce the constitution of the universe.[25]

The acceptance of national culture goes hand in hand with the acceptance of national sovereignty as divinely ordained and of established social customs as divinely sanctioned. In contrast to the universal culture which the medieval Catholic church fostered, the national churches have been the patrons of a divided, localized culture and so have accentuated the differences between nations. They have often played an important rôle in developing the barbaric racial tongue into a cultural language, as the influence of the German Bible and of the King James version especially show; they have fostered nationally differentiated arts and philosophies as founders and patrons of national "universities." In turn they have been influenced by the divided nationalist cultures and in their thought-forms as well as in their language have become illustrations of the different national psychologies. Hence the theology of Germany, and its philosophy, stand in marked contrast to the theology and philosophy of Great Britain and of America. Not only the words but the ideas that seek to clothe themselves in these symbols tend to become unintelligible to members of another cultural group. So the church becomes the victim as well as the source of national civilizations. Instead of representing a common Christian ideal and fostering mutual understanding of the disciples in all parts of the world, it becomes responsible for much of their misunderstanding of each other and supports them in their mutual suspicions and fears.

This analysis of the nationalist character of the Reformation churches should not be interpreted as denying the influence of individual leaders in determining the character of churches. After all, the German church is not only German but also Lutheran; the Scotch church is not only Scotch but also the church of John Knox. The religion of Luther, it may be said, has been as decisive in moulding German character and culture as these have been in moulding Lutheranism. The Presbyterianism of Knox, it will be maintained, has made Scotland not less than Scotland made Presbyterianism. Yet such considerations, true as they are, do not account for the varieties of religious organization and their mutual antagonism. Calvin, Knox, and Luther were far more closely related than are the churches which derive from them, and before they began to make their probably inevitable compromises with the world they were still more nearly akin. The Luther who began the Reformation belonged to mankind. He was the spiritual brother of the Hebrew Paul, the Latin Augustine, the English Wesley, as well as of the French Calvin and the Scotch Knox. But the Luther who founded the Lutheran church as a separate, nationalist denomination was a Germanized Luther, who needed to attenuate his heroic conceptions in order that German nationalism might save Christianity from its Latinic degeneracy.[26] And this was true of the other leaders whose disagreements rather than agreements with each other are remembered by the churches which glorify their names. In the end nationalism was more powerful than the common religious ideas and ideals. The churches became nations at prayer, but even in prayer Christians found it difficult to transcend the limitations of national consciousness. The kingdoms of the world became the kingdom of our Lord and of his Christ, but only by subdividing the latter along the boundaries of the former and by accommodating the rule of the divine Sovereign to the peculiar needs of his various mundane retainers.

CHAPTER SIX

SECTIONALISM AND DENOMINATIONALISM
IN AMERICA

The primary social sources of American denominationalism are to be sought in the European history
of the churches which have immigrated to the new
world. Yet many of the two hundred varieties of
Christianity which flourish in the United States were
born within its confines and many others which
derive their origin from Europe owe the development
of their present separate individuality to the operation of social forces native to the new environment.
Among the factors which have been responsible for
the continued division of European proletarian, bourgeois, and nationalist Christianity in America, for
the development of new types of conflict between
them, and for the rise of wholly American schisms,
sectionalism, the heterogeneity of an immigrant
population, and the presence of two distinct races
are of primary importance. America replaced the
horizontal lines of European class structure with the
vertical lines of a sectionalized society and continued
or originated church schisms in accordance with that
pattern of provincial organization of East and West
and North and South which underlies its economic
and political history. It brought the diverse races of
Europe, with their various religious organizations,

into a new relationship in which new kinds of accommodation and new kinds of conflict greatly modified the character of their church life. The third set of social factors which have been responsible for a great deal of denominationalism in America have arisen out of the forced migration to the New World of the African race and out of the subsequent relations of whites and Negroes.

I

The part which the sectional conflict between North and South has played in the history of church schism in America is well-known. Less obviously but not less effectively the constantly recurring strife between East and West has left its mark on religious life in the United States and has been responsible for the divergent development of a number of denominations. It is to be noted that just as North and South may represent cultural and economic forces more than geographical areas, so also the terms East and West, in this connection, designate complex social structures and movements rather than geographic sections. Throughout a large part of the eighteenth and the whole of the nineteenth century the advancing Western frontier brought forth a typical culture of its own, which not only profoundly affected the whole civilization of the United States but also came into frequent conflict with the established society of the mercantile East. It produced its own type of economic life and theory, its own kind of political practice and doctrine and created its own typical,

[136]

religious experience and expression. The result was the formation of peculiarly Western denominations. These followed partly in the tradition of the European churches of the poor but were, nevertheless, truly indigenous outgrowths of the American environment. The East, upon the other hand, clung fast to the established forms of European religious life and found itself unable to maintain unity with the frontier. Hence there came to pass a division of the churches which speciously appears to be simply the continuation of earlier European schisms, but which has its true source in the sectional differences and conflicts of American civilization.

The significance of the frontier in moulding the characteristic institutions of American society and in influencing the typical attitudes of American citizens has been compared to the significance of the Mediterranean to the Greeks in "breaking the bond of custom, offering new experiences, calling out new institutions and activities." [1] The expansive tendencies of American enterprise were fostered for centuries by the challenging opportunities offered by free land and virgin soil and by the ever-renewed possibilities for conquest and fortune. Equalitarianism in political doctrine was nurtured less in the land of Puritans and Pilgrims than in the Western settlements, where the common struggle for existence allowed no distinctions between high and low and where success attended effort rather than the fortune of inherited privilege. The love of liberty was also bred on the border; "complex society," says Turner, "is precipitated by the wilderness into a kind of primitive organization, based on the family. The tendency is anti-social. It produces antipathy to control, and particularly to any direct control. The frontier individualism has from the beginning promoted democracy." [2] To this influence of the wilderness must be added the effect of freeland, which made freeholders with inalienable rights out of city apprentices or immigrant peasants and so furnished them with a foundation for an individual sense of worth as well as with a basis for the construction of democratic institutions. Furthermore, the frontier was selective. Its opportunities and dangers attracted the independent and the fearless as well as many a rebel against established order. [3] Again, so it is maintained, the national consciousness as contrasted with the rival provincialisms of the early colonies had its cradle in the West, where men from all the sections and from many European countries needed to work out their common salvation in conflict with forest, prairie, and marshland, or with French and Indian warriors.

For our present point of view the common stamp which the frontier may have given to the American character is less significant than the division which it undoubtedly brought forth. On the basis of its economic system and its peculiar economic needs it produced political and social theories which were directly opposed to the doctrines and customs of the East. Hence wave after wave of frontier revolt broke over the older East as frontier after frontier nurtured new groups of Western radicals. "In each case the men broken by one wave had been among the leaders of the last, and the clearest voice of frontier guidance came from the freshest frontier group." [4] So Jeffersonianism, Jacksonianism, and Lincolnian Republicanism owed much of their character to the spirit of the rising West. The conflict between the frontier and the coast was largely due to the opposing interests of agricultural and commercial, of debtor and creditor, societies. In part it was based on the contrast of sectional interests, as in the question of the location of trade routes, or of social institutions, as in the case of the terms of land tenure. But the most important cause of actual division was the difference in social and political philosophy which arose out of these economic divergencies. The frontier, in each period, developed a higher appreciation of "natural rights" and a more democratic type of local government than the older settlement possessed. Indeed, this conflict of political theory antedated the rise of the new states of the West by many years and had come to expression in the division of parties during and immediately after the Revolution. [5]

Political and economic strife between East and West was aggravated by cultural differences. The refinements and arts of urban society have ever been the subject of rural ridicule while the uncouth naïveté of the farmer and woodsman have always seemed offensive to those whose lives are surrounded and conditioned by the products of industry and art. The difficulty of providing adequate education for the poor, scattered communities of the frontier and the lack of communication between the isolated settlements contributed to the cultural differentiation of the West. The influence of European immigration was another source of frontier individuality; for as ever new tides of migrants came to America they found the soil of the East pre-empted by earlier comers. These regarded themselves as the appointed guardians of the country and were prone to look with contempt on the foreigners whom they sent to garrison the frontier.[6] For all these reasons and many corollary ones the established order of the East found itself in frequent conflict with a revolutionary West.

The same causes which brought on political and economic conflict promoted religious controversy and schism. For the churches of America, no less than those of Europe, have often been more subject to the influence of provincial or class environment than to the persuasions of a common gospel. Under the influence of sectional conflicts religious schisms resulted more frequently, arose earlier, and lasted longer than did political divisions. Eastern and Western, Northern and Southern states, despite all party battles and sanguine conflict, have been able to re-establish their political unity more quickly than Eastern and Western, Northern and Southern churches have been able to reaffirm their ecclesiastical integrity.

The religious conflicts of the established societies of the East with the free civilization of the frontier arose out of the same circumstances that brought forth political and economic strife. The social conditions, which in the one case fostered the Federalist and later Republican temper and theory of government and in the other case the Jeffersonian and Jacksonian attitude and views of political organization, nurtured contrasting theories and practices of religious experience and expression as well as of ecclesiastical organization in the churches. The religion of the urban, commercial East tended to take on or to retain the typical features of all bourgeois or national religion—a polity corresponding to the order and character of class organized society, an intellectual conception of the content of faith, an ethics reflecting the needs and evaluations of a stable and commercial citizenry, a sober, ritualistic type of religious expression. The religion of the West, on the other hand, accepted or produced anew many of the characteristics of the faith of the disinherited, for the psychology of the frontier corresponds in many respects to the psychology of the revolutionary poor. This is especially true of the emotional character of religious experience, which seems to be required in the one case as in the other. The isolation of frontier life fostered craving for companionship, suppressed the gregarious tendency and so subjected the lonely settler to the temptations of crowd suggestion to an unusual degree. In the camp-meeting and in the political gathering formal, logical discourse was of no avail, while the "language of excitement" called forth enthusiastic response. In addition to the isolation of the frontiersman other influences inclined him to make an uncritical emotional response to religious stimulation. The reduction of life on the border to the bare fundamentals of physical and social existence, the dearth of intellectual stimulation and the lack of those effective inhibitions of emotional expression which formal education cultivates, the awesome manifestations of nature, the effects of which were not checked by the sense of safety permanent dwellings and the nearness of other men convey—all these made the settler subject to the feverish phenomena of revivalism.[7]

The religion of the frontier was further akin to the faith of the poor in the love of democracy which was expressed in it. Among the poor the desire for individual experience and responsibility in religion and for the religious support of their efforts toward political enfranchisement were brought forth in reaction against the long denial of their human rights. On the frontier, conversely, the enjoyment of economic and political liberty fostered the desire for similar privileges in religion, while the great interest in the retention of individual rights in every sphere naturally sought in faith the justification of practice. Furthermore, the same individualism which resented all absentee control in political and economic life and which prompted the Westerner to seek a personal religion in the immediacy of experience caused him to look with suspicion upon all administration of religion by superior powers ordained of God or of men. Hence lay preaching and preaching by men who, though ordained, were not separated from their fellows by the marks of superior education and culture, were favored on the frontier as they were among the disinherited. This democratic attitude also came to expression in the sectarian organization of the religious community. The churches of the frontier tended to be voluntaristic organizations, in harmony with the other social structures of the individualistic society and in conformity with the conception of religion as immediate and individual experience. The frontier influenced dogma and ethics also. The relaxation and liberation which adventurers from the East enjoyed when they found themselves on the border, free not only from the compulsions of legal restraint but also from the watchful surveillance of their neighbors, tended to break down much of their customary morality. Complaints against drunkenness, gambling, and sexual license, as well as against the profanation of the Sabbath and the prevalence of profanity, abound in the accounts of Eastern visitors to the frontier. This relaxation largely determined the character of the conversion which took place when religion struck home. Revivals under these circumstances were true revivals of those inhibitions which had been only partly overcome in a generation or two of frontier life and which continued in their suppression to foster a sense of guilt beneath the brave front of carelessness. The ethics which was prized under these circumstances was the ethics of individual morality and the negative ethics of restraint from the typical sins of the border. In this respect there was a marked difference between

the moral ideals of the frontier and those of the
religious poor; where the latter were social, growing
out of the urban and industrial solidarity of labor
and prizing sympathy and justice, the former were
individualistic, rising out of the isolation of the settler and exalting self-reliant attitudes as well as personal probity and purity.[8]

The sense of individual responsibility which was
nurtured by the self-dependent life of the frontier
may have had some influence on doctrine in addition
to the obvious emphasis which resulted from emotional religious experience. On the whole Arminianism, with its belief in the co-operative activity of
man in the work of salvation, seems more at home on
the frontier than does predestinarian Calvinism.
Yet the lines between East and West were not sharply
drawn on this issue and it was the character of the
emphasis more than the type of doctrine which distinguished one section from the other. Calvinist
orthodoxy presided over the awakening on the frontier of New England while Arminianism prevailed
on the coast. In Kentucky and Tennessee, Arminian
Methodism and Arminianized Presbyterianism opposed the orthodox doctrine of the established society. The Arminian Baptists of New England became Calvinists when they migrated to the Southwest.
The religion of the frontier or the religion of the
established society could be nurtured, it appears, on
rival types of doctrine. In the equalitarian atmosphere of the West the doctrine that there were no elect
naturally won a response but so did the teaching

that election had nothing to do with worldly fortune and that the rough-hewn, illiterate son of the border might just as well be a divinely chosen vessel as the cultured gentleman of respectable society. Under these circumstances the shifting emphases of doctrine were probably more often the result of strategy in the denominational wars on the border and in the party strife within the church than of the preference of the frontier for one or the other type of faith. It remains true that the same type of religion was fostered now by Calvinism and now by Arminianism.[9]

II

Almost all of the churches of America have, at some time or another, lived on the frontier, and almost all of them have retained some of the marks of the character which it sought to impress upon them. In a very general sense it is true that under the influence of frontier conditions the churches of Europe after migrating to America have tended to become sects, and that with the passing of the frontier and with the establishment of ordered society the sects of Europe and America have tended to become churches. Yet the influence of the frontier on the denominations has been very unequal. Some of them, by virtue of a rigid constitution acquired in earlier history, were able to resist the influence of border life or were unable to adapt themselves to it; others, again by virtue of their earlier character, were attracted to the frontier as a fitting field for their labors and readily adjusted themselves to its needs;

some denominations, from the beginning of their American history, sought their membership only among those European classes or nationalities which found their home in the mercantile East or in the semi-aristocratic, plantation South; others, again, needed to follow their European adherents to the wilderness and to remain alien to the interests of the established society; still other denominations were native born, having originated in frontier religious revolts. Heredity and environment sometimes conspired but sometimes fought against each other to conserve or to change denominational character, to continue denominational differences or to unite groups which had previously been sundered.

Of the denominations which were confined to the settled area of the early East both as a result of their constitution and of the cultural character of their membership the Anglican or Protestant Episcopal Church is a typical example. The same factors which prevented it, in England, from fully accepting the Wesleyan revival operated in America to keep it aloof from the vivid, popular religion of the frontier. As the church of the Southern plantation aristocracy, of English bureaucracy and mercantile groups in the ports and capitals of the colonies, it represented those interests of which the frontier was most suspicious. In Virginia it lost the border population to Baptists, Methodists, and Presbyterians.[10] In Maryland, where also it was the established church, "the Methodists . . . swept the country; . . . the enthusiasm of the New Lights and other itinerant preachers found a hearty, if ignorant, response; . . . Quakers and Presbyterians from Pennsylvania gathered large numbers into their respective folds." [11] In the northern colonies the obvious connection of the church with the Loyalists of 1776 brought on its almost complete ruin. When it was re-established as an American Episcopal church after the Revolution it gained, indeed, in vitality but did not change its character as the church of English middle classes in the East.[12] It retained its sober, ritualist forms despite all the temptations offered by the frontier spirit of the new nation and became the refuge of many who were offended by the emotional enthusiasm of the revivals which, originating in the West, spread also to the East.[13]

The Congregationalism of New England, in contrast to Episcopalianism, appeared to be endowed by constitution and training for religious work on the frontier. From its origin as a church of the poor in the early seventeenth century it had maintained the sectarian principle of organization and an apparently democratic character. On the first frontier of the new world, Massachusetts Bay, the development of these characteristics had been encouraged by the social organization in isolated communities and the Puritan majority had conformed to the pattern of the Separatist minority.[14] But in few other respects was this early Puritan Congregationalism sympathetic to the needs of the border communities which began to take on definitely frontier character a century after the founding of New England. Its characteristics were not those of the religiously naïve, but those of established and cultured social classes. Puritanism rather than Separatism gave it its chief endowment. The early Puritan colonies "contained men of humble position, it is true, but their leaders were from good station in England, many of them of the country gentry, men of wealth, character and education. Their ministers . . . were the peers in learning and ability of any in the Puritan wing of the Church of England. . . . Probably no colony in the history of European emigration was superior to that of Massachusetts in wealth, station or capacity." [15] Emotionalism in religion was abhorrent to these learned clergymen and substantial citizens; lay preaching was associated in their minds with an equally detested radicalism in political and religious theory. The lack of truly democratic principles among the Puritans has been pointed out. Nor were they loth, as soon as settled conditions prevailed, to give up a sectarianism which had been forced upon them by the American situation rather than espoused as a matter of principle. The Half-Way Covenant and Stoddardeanism provided for the establishment of a church in which membership eventually was based on social relationship and inherited by birth rather than conditioned on individual experience and voluntary decision.[16]

.The attitude of this established and well-ordered faith toward the new frontiers which were soon formed far beyond Massachusetts Bay was expressed at an early day by Cotton Mather who warned those who swarm into the new settlements that they were on the "wrong side of the hedge," and that for the sake of earthly gain they were likely to be driven to the wall with Balaam and to perish from lack of vision.[17] In the antagonism between the Puritan towns and Rhode Island some of the same factors entered in which in later days brought schism between the churches of the East and the West. But the first real crisis in New England Congregationalism between the established society and the frontier occurred in the Great Awakening. The revival began in 1734-35 on the frontier of Massachusetts and Connecticut, in towns, which though they had been settled many years before, were still the outposts of civilization, facing the wilderness between the Connecticut and the Hudson, and far removed from the influences of the Old World and of the settled society on the Bay.[18] Under Whitefield's preaching, it is true, the Awakening eventually reached the seaboard towns also and there attracted primarily the lower economic classes, but it prospered most in the interior.

The familiar characteristics of this first religious revival on American soil have been frequently described. Fervent preaching, rich in images, nervous disturbances, spreading from person to person, from town to town, the sudden accessions of peace—these were quite similar to the phenomena of the almost contemporary Methodist revival in England. The Awakening remained under the leadership of a clergy which had been trained in the frontier parsonages and at Yale; lay preaching was not largely practiced; but sectarian organization was the inevitable outcome of the whole movement with its emphasis on conversion.[19]

The clergy of the older settlements—especially those of Boston and vicinity but also those of the older towns in Connecticut—were alike offended by the emotional crudities of the converted and the undiplomatic zeal of the preachers. The division between Old Lights and New Lights, as the parties opposing and favoring the revival were called, was aggravated but not caused by the Calvinism of the frontier revival preachers under the leadership of Jonathan Edwards and by the accusations of Arminianism made against the clergy of the conservative East. The points at issue in the meetings of the Congregational pastors were not so much doctrinal as practical. In 1741 the General Consociation in Connecticut and in 1743 the annual convention of Massachusetts Bay pastors bore testimony against those who "look upon what are called secret impulses upon their minds without due regard to the written word, the rule of their conduct, that none are converted but such as know they are converted and the time when" and condemned the "ungoverned passions," "the disorderly tumults and indecent behavior" of the revivals. They were equally shocked by the itineracy and by "the heinous invasion of the ministerial office" by "private persons of no education and but low attainments in knowledge and in the great doctrines of the gospel" and by "the spirit and practice of separation from the particular flocks

[150]

to which persons belong, to join themselves with and to support lay exhorters or itinerants." [20]   In Connecticut the ruling Old Side party prevailed on the legislature to pass "an Act for regulating abuses and correcting disorders in ecclesiastical affairs" which was directed against itineracy and lay preaching by exhorters who "have no ecclesiastical character or license to preach." [21]

The outcome of this conflict between the faith of the frontier or of the poor and the religion of the established communities was schism.   The radical wing of the revival movement was constituted by "those wild people, called Separatists"—in Jonathan Edwards' phrase—and these formed independent churches on the sectarian principle in many parts of New England—chiefly, however, in eastern Connecticut.   They were mostly people in humble circumstances, "warm-hearted, spiritually-minded, though ignorant persons who had been profoundly touched by the revival" and now opposed the Half-Way Covenant, "held that an educated ministry or premeditated sermons were unnecessary, attached great value to visions and to religious excitement in public meetings" and believed that the church "could discern by spiritual intuition who were the real Christians who alone should constitute its membership." [22]   These Separatist churches met the fate of most other conventicles of the poor, for the allied Puritan hierocracy and state subjected them to persecutions which, coupled with internal dissension, soon brought on their decline.[23]   The heir of the movement, however, was the Baptist church, which, similar as it was in character to this Separatist movement, not only took the new churches under its wing but also attracted many individuals who had been affected by the revival but had retained membership in the Congregational churches. Henceforth the Baptists became the exponents of the religion of the frontier in New England.[24]

The Congregational church was profoundly affected by the Awakening and the schism, but, although it returned to the stricter sectarian practices of its earlier years in the New World and adopted revival preaching as a regular method of church work, it by no means became a church of the frontier or the poor; it remained aloof from the religious movements of the West. For the next century and longer it continued to be a provincial New England denomination which made its appeal to the middle classes of established communities and was unable to maintain, in the long run, an effective contact either with the frontier and the poor or with the metropolitan aristocracy of wealth and intellect. The former groups found their religious home with the Baptists, the latter with the Episcopalians and Unitarians. Congregationalism was, it is true, extended to the frontier in the Western Reserve and it followed New Englanders to other Western states but its ministrations were primarily acceptable to those who had been trained in its traditions prior to their migration westward and many even of these forsook their earlier faith for the frontier religion of the Baptists and

Methodists. Congregationalism sent consecrated missionaries to the new territories and was responsible for the founding of many Western colleges; it supported home missionary work with exceptional generosity; but the fruit of these labors was often gathered by denominations who were more akin in spirit to the character of the frontier. The widespread feeling in the older Congregational churches that their faith could not thrive in unformed communities may itself have been partly responsible for the fact that it did not do so,[25] but it remains true that this denomination achieved success only in established and mercantile societies. It was allied politically with the Federalism against which the West revolted, and it regarded the religious and the political proclivities of the frontier with equal suspicion. Timothy Dwight, leader of New England Congregationalism that he was, doubtless expressed the attitude of many members of his group, when he inveighed with Cotton Mather against the frontiersmen who were "too idle; too talkative; too passionate; too prodigal; and too shiftless to acquire either property or character." "They are usually possessed," he believed, "in their own view of uncommon wisdom; understand medical science, politics and religion better than those who have studied them all their life; and although they manage their own concerns worse than other men, feel perfectly satisfied that they could manage those of the nation far better than the agents to whom they are committed by the public." [26] So political and religious conservatism combined to do battle with political and religious radicalism; New England Federalist Congregationalists stood over against Western Jeffersonian Methodists and Baptists, and the cleavage of churches once more reflected the underlying cleavages of sectionalized society.

Despite some changes brought about by the *rapprochement* of East and West through the organization of the Republican party, the fortunes of the Civil War and the passing of the frontier, Congregationalism has remained a church of established cities and towns. There it has found that type of educated middle class, usually of New England origin, which feels at home in its atmosphere of highly respectable learning, doctrine, piety and ethics. Under the influence of this class alliance it has undergone the changes through which most other churches of the bourgeoisie have passed. Its doctrine and its ethics have been accommodated to the culture, the needs and the interests of its clientele. Though it produced such a prophet of the larger fellowship as Washington Gladden, though its liberal spirit impels it to seek the union of all denominations, it remains conditioned by the social character of a special group, and continues to present less than a universal appeal.

III

The history of the Presbyterian Church in America is similar in many respects to that of Congregationalism. In this case also the church of an established European society found it impossible to adapt its character to the needs and interests of the frontier, suffering schism and loss as a result. There are interesting differences, however, between the two denominations. Presbyterianism with its firm ecclesiastical structure and its hard and fast dogmas was much farther removed from the democratic forms and the interest in local control prevailing in frontier social life than was Congregationalism. Yet it made a somewhat more successful, though still inadequate, adaptation to the conditions of the border. As the church of the Scotch-Irish it was, geographically, a frontier church throughout the first century of its existence on American soil. The Ulster immigration, coming to the New World after the coast lands had been settled, was forced to find its home on the frontier of New England and the Middle colonies. So the church was faced with the necessity of adjusting itself to the religious character of a people in whom the wilderness called forth not only the relaxation of moral and religious discipline but also the need for an emotional rebirth. Conflict between tradition and the new spirit was inevitable. In view of the rigid constitution of Presbyterianism it was probably also inevitable that there should be schism, but not before Presbyterianism had been strongly influenced by its new environment.

The first intimation of any difficulty came with the Great Awakening. The leaders of the revival party in the Presbyterian church were men who had come under the influence of frontier conditions in New England and New Jersey—especially the Tennents, who had been educated in the Log College at Neshaminy. Their conflict with the anti-revival party has often been represented as due to the antagonism between New England Puritans, who had migrated to the Middle colonies where they had joined the Presbyterian church, and Scotch-Irish who maintained a conservative attitude in religious practice.[27] It was, however, more truly a conflict between two generations of Scotch-Irish, between an immigrant generation nurtured in Europe and the first native-born, frontier-bred generation. The leaders of the radical party in the church were not New Englanders but Scotch-Irish frontier preachers. The issues between the two parties were similar to those which had been raised in New England Congregationalism by the revival. The "Old Side," conservative, or European party charged its opponents, the revivalists, with holding "heterodox and anarchic principles" in denying the authority of Presbyteries "to oblige their dissenting members," with "making irregular irruptions upon congregations to which they have no immediate relation," with believing the ministerial call to be transmitted not by ordination but by "some invisible motions and workings of the spirit, which none can be conscious or sensible of but the person himself," with "industrially working on the passions and affections of weak minds, as to cause them to cry out in a hideous manner and fall down in convulsion-like fits." [28] The revival party accused the conservatives of being unregenerate Christians, blind leaders of the blind. The schism which resulted lasted until 1758 by which time the Old Side leaders had passed on, a frontier-bred clergy had assumed control and frontier methods had prevailed. So the church became for a time a frontier church, at least so far as its iron-clad structure permitted. The "demand for regenerate church membership not only set aside the judgment of charity of the reformed churches, but introduced the fashion of speaking of the adult communicants as the only 'members of the church' and of treating its baptized children as outside pagans, exempt even from its discipline." [29] The position of the ministry became less separate and formal while the sacramental theory changed from the institutional conception to the theory prevailing in the voluntaristic sects, that the rites were professions of grace and tokens of fellowship. [30] With the adoption of these modifications and with the westward migration of the Scotch-Irish the Presbyterian church, more than any other in America, became the church of the frontier during the latter half of the eighteenth century. [31]

Yet the rigidity of its constitutional system was such that the West was unable to bend it into conformity with the pattern of its religious life without fracturing the unity of the church. [32] Not to be denied in its insistence on a faith conformable to its spirit and its needs, the frontier rebelled against the established order, dividing Presbyterianism into Eastern and Western branches. The results of this impact of pioneer faith upon the church are recorded in the histories of the Stoneite or New Light schism, of the organization of the Cumberland Presbyterian church, of the development of Shaker communities in Kentucky and Ohio, of the loss of many members of the Presbyterian denomination to Methodist, Baptist and Disciple churches and, in part, of the schism of the parent church in Old and New School Assemblies. In so doctrinal a church as the Presbyterian it was inevitable that these various party conflicts should assume a theological character. The question most often in dispute, at least upon the surface, was the question of Arminianism or Calvinism. Indeed, the tendency toward a type of doctrine which assigned some share to human effort in the process of salvation and which, denying the dogma of election, seemed to place all men on more evident equality before God was a symptomatic expression of the American and especially the frontier spirit while orthodox Calvinism was more akin to the spirit of European and all established society. The fundamental differences of attitude between Eastern and Western parties in the church, however, were more evidently expressed in the conflicts about polity and about methods of evangelization than in the doctrinal disputes.

The Cumberland schism offers the best illustration of the fact that it was a frontier faith which rebelled against the parent church and a frontier type of religious piety which the older branch of the denomination was unable to include within its established scheme. The issues between the contending groups, in addition to the issue of doctrine, were once more the questions of emotional rebirth, of an educated or of an uneducated but converted clergy, of sectarian organization. The ordination or licensure of uneducated laymen whose piety and evangelistic fervor recommended them to the missionary preachers in the Cumberland settlements on the far frontier of the new territories, resulted in the censure of these preachers by the Synod of Kentucky, in the establishment of the Cumberland Presbytery and in the eventual separation of this body from fellowship with the parent church. The doctrinal question was involved, in so far as the question of licensing uneducated preachers was a question of admitting to the ministry men whose attitude to the confession was influenced more by the practical education afforded by the frontier than by the logical devices of theology. The differences between the two groups were also expressed in their contrasting attitudes toward the camp-meeting revivals, which the preachers from the Cumberland heartily championed but which the members of the older church regarded with great suspicion. Furthermore, the tendency of the frontier preachers to organize their churches as societies on the sectarian principle may have furnished another cause for dissatisfaction on the part of the established clergy.[33]

The rise of the Cumberland church had been preceded by a similar schism of the Springfield Presbytery—another frontier group in the Southwest which broke away from the Presbyterian church in 1803 and in the following year sought to organize itself under the leadership of B. W. Stone as an independent denomination, the Christian Church. In this instance the schismatic group represented, to an even greater extent than did the Cumberland Presbytery, an emotional type of frontier faith. It revolted against all creeds and sought to establish a simple, lay Christianity on a biblical basis.[34] The extreme development of this religion of the border was found among the Shakers who brought into the Kentucky area the millenarian, communistic ideas and the ecstatic forms of the Old World religions of the poor. They attracted the radical wing of the frontier movement, including two pastors and many lay members of the Stoneite group.[35] Other sects of a similar sort flourished for a brief time in the wake of the revival and of the advancing frontier and, by contagion in the excitable atmosphere of nineteenth-century America, infected the whole nation with the spirit of utopianism, religious impressionism, and emotional mobility.[36] One such group, that of the Mormons, under able leadership, was able to survive and to form a really distinct and important religious denomination.

These extreme effects which were produced on the religious life by the frontier environment were probably not the most important results of the conflict of East and West, so far as the Presbyterian church was concerned. Its loss of members to the Cumberland church, to the frontier denominations of the Methodists, Baptists, and Disciples of Christ was of greater significance and no less indicative of the social character of the denominationalism fostered by the cultural cleavage. The defection to these other churches of thousands of Scotch-Irish, who constituted by heredity the natural clientele of Presbyterianism, and the consequent rise of these denominations were undoubtedly due to the influence of frontier conditions and to the failure of the European and Eastern church to adapt itself to the needs of the West. "Of the descendants of the Ulster Presbyterians," Thompson says in his history of Presbyterianism in America, "probably not much above a third are today Presbyterian. However large the membership and extensive the influence of the church, therefore, it cannot be called successful even in holding its own, much less in aggressive power." Analyzing the causes of its insufficiency he points to the scholastic shape in which the doctrines of the church were presented in confessions and catechisms, to the influence of these on teaching and preaching, and to the rigidity of the church's policy in ministerial education, which judged the needs of the frontier by the standards of Philadelphia and insisted on "making men gentlemen before it made them ministers." [37]

After these revolutionary days, during which Presbyterianism lost so large a part of its territory, of its membership and its commanding position in American church life, it tended more than ever to seek its strength in the established communities of the East or of the older West. In the great schism of 1837, when the Old School and the New School divided, some of the same factors which were present in the Kentucky schisms came again to light. They were complicated by the difficulty of reconciling the differences between those churches which had been influenced most strongly by the Congregational tradition and those whose customs and thought-forms were derived more directly from the Scotch Reformation. From the social point of view the New School of Presbyterianism represented the Western branch of Congregationalism more than a wing of Scotch-Irish Presbyterianism.[38] The healing of the schism as of the earlier divisions came with the passing of the frontier and the frontier spirit to a remoter West and with the mutual accommodation of opposing parties to a new national culture which, though it continued to bear the traces of pioneer days, had substituted the established customs and institutional interests of matured society for the sectarianism and emotionalism of the erstwhile "wild West."

The division between the frontier and the established society had its lasting influence upon other churches besides the Congregational and the Presbyterian. The Reformed Church in the United States and the Lutheran church, both representative of German established churches, had become frontier denominations by force of circumstance, when their membership in migrating to America had found its best opportunities on the western borders of the early colonies. On the frontier of Pennsylvania these Germans were subjected to the influences not only of many sectaries from the homeland—Dunkards, Schwenkfelders and similar groups—but also of those primitive conditions which played havoc in Kentucky with the sober stability of the Scotch-Irish. For a time the pietist evangelists of the two German churches were able to hold their own but when the influence of the Methodist revival was added to the other tendencies toward sectarian religion a schism between the frontier and established society seemed again to be inevitable. The result was the organization of the church of the United Brethren in Christ and the Evangelical Church. These groups represented among the Germans the same spirit and principles which were represented among the Scotch-Irish by the Cumberland, Christian, and Disciple churches. The cultural differences between the Eastern and Western wings of German Protestantism as in the case of Scotch Protestantism, became evident in the unequal influence of revivalism on the two groups, in widely varying standards of ministerial education and of doctrinal subscription and in a considerable disparity of interest in education in general.[39]

Out of the religious movement on the frontier in the eighteenth and early nineteenth century there arose, in this way, a considerable number of sects which divided from their parent bodies because divergent social and economic conditions had emphasized different religious needs and expressions. The movement was in part due to Wesleyan inspiration, but the frontier furnished the conditions under which this inspiration became effective on the mass. It was in part due to the leadership of individuals, to the Tennents and Edwards, to Stone and McGready, to Otterbein and Albright; but it was the frontier which produced these leaders and gave them their opportunity, just as in the political sphere it produced Jackson and Lincoln and the conditions which inspired response to their appeal. It cannot be maintained that every Westerner was affected by the frontier type of religious faith, nor that every Easterner held fast to the traditions; "many a tinker," says Beard, "cheered for King Charles"; and many a pioneer prayed fervently for the preservation of the Westminster Confession. Many an Easterner, on the other hand, was profoundly influenced by the spirit which spread from the frontier through the whole country. Yet when the movement of American denominationalism is surveyed as a whole, apart from the loyalties and defections of solitary individuals, the conflict between East and West clearly stands out as a major cause of division, and its effects on the church are again indicative of the sociological rather than of the theological character of schism.

CHAPTER SEVEN

SECTIONALISM AND DENOMINATIONALISM
(*Continued*)

I

The conflicts between the cultures of the frontier, agricultural West and of the established, commercial East did not come to a close with the rise of Jeffersonian democracy and with the religious movements of 1800 to 1810. They continued throughout the remainder of the era of settlement, though they were obscured for a time by the crisis between the North and the South. No such spectacular revolts of frontier faith as those of the Cumberland and the Springfield Presbyteries occurred in the ensuing years. Spasmodic revival movements and evanescent sects sprang forth from the Western soil year by year for many a decade. But the necessity for revolts on a large scale had stopped with the establishment of three great frontier churches, which anticipated the needs of the Western settlers and drew them away from their earlier loyalties one by one rather than in secessionist groups. These three denominations—the outstanding examples of frontier religion—were the churches of the Methodists and Baptists and the Disciples of Christ.

By virtue of the affinity between the religious

movements of the poor and those of the frontier, Methodists and Baptists found the advancing Western settlements of America congenial soil for their methods of cultivation. Their conceptions of conversion, of the ministry, and of sectarian polity both influenced and were influenced by the religious spirit of the pioneers. The Disciples' church, however, was of native growth and represented a frontier effort to gather into a single group the religious people who, coming from many churches and traditions, had been moulded to a common pattern by the West.

Prior, indeed, to the rise of these three churches the Society of Friends functioned as a frontier denomination. In the colonial era it occupied not only the cities of Pennsylvania but was represented to a considerable extent in the scattered settlements on the border from Rhode Island to Georgia. Before the immigration of the Scotch-Irish Presbyterians and the coming of Methodist and Baptist itinerants, it was the Quaker missionary who rode the lonely trails of the back country, holding religious meetings wherever he could gather a few Friends together. The democratic and lay character of the faith of Fox and Woolman made a strong appeal to the frontier and its influence was far greater than the numerical strength of the denomination indicated. For the sectarian peculiarities of Quakerism and its high ethical demands prevented many who had been profoundly affected by its spirit from making the final commitment to its principles. The lack of an aggressive policy, the passive and quietistic attitude of "the middle age of Quakerism," and the "tendency to run to form" rather than to "abide in the power and the life," were also responsible for the failure of this first frontier church to maintain its leadership. But its contribution to the religious character of the Western settlements was demonstrated in the harvests. reaped by Baptists and Methodists in the regions first tilled by Quaker missionaries.[1]

Greater success awaited the Baptists, whose churches were not always the heirs of a European tradition but frequently the native-born children of the frontier religious movements. As immigrants they had established themselves on the New England frontier, in Rhode Island, where their sectarian principles had been nurtured in isolation from the established society of the New World as well as of the Old. Religious and cultural conditions combined to erect a wall of division between Massachusetts Bay, New York and Connecticut on the one hand and the Providence and Narragansett plantations on the other. Still, it was an Old World division which kept Baptists and Calvinists apart during the first century. Rhode Island, in the regard of New York and New England was not so much a frontier as "the receptacle of all sorts of riff-raff people," "nothing else than the sewer (latrina) of New England."[2] The Baptist church came into its own as an American and frontier church in the days of the Great Awakening, when it became the refuge of those whose frontier faith made continued connection with established Congregationalism difficult. These found in the religious ideals and practices of the Baptists the very features which the logic of their own experiences seemed to require of a church—the consciously experienced conversion of adults, lay preaching and sectarian organization. Many of the "New Light" and Separatist churches entered the Baptist fold and individual conversions to its faith were numerous.[3] The leader of the Baptists in this period, Isaac Backus, was himself one of these Separatists. The increase of the church in the years following the Great Awakening indicates the extent to which it profited by a movement it had done little to promote. In Massachusetts the six Baptist churches of 1740 had increased to thirty by 1768 and to ninety-two by 1790; in Rhode Island during the same period the comparable figures were eleven, thirty-six and thirty-eight; the four Baptist churches of Connecticut in 1740 had increased to fifty-five by 1790.[4] In Maine the frontier sect of Free-Will Baptists achieved a similar success. As the settlements pushed ever further westward the Baptist church seemed to become the frontier branch of Congregationalism. In Western New York, after 1763, it served not only the New England Separatists but also drew into its fellowship many settlers from New England who had remained true to Congregationalism in the earlier environment.[5] In Virginia, the Carolinas and Georgia Baptists, representing New England Separatism on the one hand and the General Baptists of England on the other hand, achieved remarkable success on frontiers left unoccupied by the established

Anglican church.[6] Differences of opinion between these two branches were natural, in view of their past histories, and friction was inevitable at this time as it was later on in Kentucky and Tennessee. Under the common influence of the new environment, however, the two groups soon adjusted themselves to each other and formed one church, save in isolated communities where the early distinctions and local differences have been preserved down to the present time.[7]

Its greatest success awaited the Baptist church on the new frontier of 1800. Kentucky and Tennessee and the adjacent sections of the West attracted thousands of Baptists from the older settlements, for their economic and cultural condition was generally such that they had much to gain and little to lose by risking their future on the promise and the uncertainty of the frontier. But the rapid growth of the denomination in the Southwest was not due only to the immigration of its adherents. It increased even more rapidly at the expense of those Eastern churches which were unable to meet the demands of the West, especially during the years of the great revival. In Kentucky the period between 1792 and 1812 was marked by the increase of the number of Baptist churches from forty-two to two hundred and eighty-five and of the membership from 3,095 to 22,694. In Tennessee during the same period twenty-one organizations with nine hundred members increased to one hundred fifty-six churches with 11,325 members.[8] This growth must be compared with "the almost total desolation of the Presbyterian churches in Kentucky and part of Tennessee" during the latter part of the same period.[9] From this new center Baptist propaganda was carried southward and westward, keeping pace with the advancing frontier until the settlement of the Far West, beyond the Missouri, issued a challenge which the church seemed unable to meet. The last frontier was one of a new order, with which the methods of the old frontier apparently could not deal. But on the old frontiers the Baptist denomination established itself as the church of the agriculturalists and small tradesmen, who succeeded the pioneers. The conservatism of established rural and village society took the place of the emotional fervor of earlier days. The revival became part of a new ritual, which called forth the more or less traditional response of conversion. The warmth of untheological but inspired preachers gave way to the conservatism of a consecrated and institutional-minded though still untheological clergy. The practice of restricting the membership to the regenerate, experienced adult Christians was adjusted to the requirements of succeeding generations by the virtual acceptance of the church type of organization, by the establishment of Sunday schools, the consecration of children, and the gradually increasing practice of open communion.

The American denomination, which, above all others, became the frontier church in the nineteenth century and which profited most by the religious spirit of the West was the Methodist Episcopal Church. Beginning just before the Revolution in humble fashion among the poor of the Eastern cities, its promise of growth was not great in the early years of its activity in the colonies. It was an American branch of the English movement and without the frontier its significance as a church would scarcely have been greater eventually than that of Methodism in England. It might, indeed, have been considerably less, for the reaction of patriotic sentiment against a movement which was so closely related to Anglicanism and which carried the incubus of Wesley's fulminations on the subject of American independence almost destroyed it during the War of Independence. But given a free hand by Wesley's well-advised appointment of American superintendents, Methodism soon found its proper sphere on the borders of the colonies. With its fervent piety, its lay preaching, its early sectarian polity, it accorded well with the spirit of the West, while the itineracy and the circuit system were admirable devices for the evangelization of the frontier.[10] While it is true that the centralization of control in the Wesleyan church ran counter to the provincial and individualistic temper of isolated pioneer communities, yet this form of organization gave Methodism direction and concentration of energy which the loose polity of the Baptist movement lacked. This centralization of control was a corollary of the itineracy; in combination they constituted a missionary strategy which conquered the West.[11]

Before Methodism could become a frontier church, however, it needed to relinquish part of its inheritance as the child of Anglicanism and the autocratic Wesley. When it was established in America as an independent church the new rôle it assumed seemed to require the adoption of the ecclesiastical forms prevailing in the Episcopal church. The use of the prayer-book was one of these. "For some time the preachers [of the Methodist Church] generally read prayers on the Lord's Day," said an early historian of American Methodism, "and in some cases the preachers read part of the morning service on Wednesdays and Fridays; but some who had been long accustomed to pray extempore were unwilling to adopt this new plan, being fully satisfied that they could pray better and with more devotion while their eyes were shut than they could with their eyes open." Dislike of liturgical forms on the part of a large majority of the membership combined with this predilection of the clergy for extempore prayers and "after a few years the Prayer-Book was laid aside." [12] With the Prayer-Book went the vestments with which Asbury desired to dignify his own episcopal rank and the knee-breeches which he wished the clergy to don. The preachers who had been recruited from the democratic ranks continued to wear the trousered habiliments of republicanism.[13] It was not the least of Methodism's advantages on the border that its missionaries were distinguished in no way from the people with whom they dealt, save in the fervor of their piety and in the purity of their lives.

But more important adjustments than these needed to be made to the democratic spirit of the new country and, especially, of the West. Wesley had intended the American church to be subject to as autocratic a régime as were the English societies and he expected his newly appointed bishops to exercise their office without reference to other control than his own. The dictatorial character of Asbury might well have agreed with this plan; yet that great leader's training in the New World's spirit and his own insight were sufficient to cause him to overrule this plan by securing from the conference his own election as superintendent. Methodism retained strong, aristocratic features, especially in its long refusal to allow lay representatives to participate in the conferences, but it was a constitutional aristocracy and the preachers were not so distinguished from the people as a separate class that the clerical government of the churches appeared to be a violation of democratic principles. Despite the fact that Asbury often expressed an autocratic spirit, he nevertheless accommodated the character of the church to the new environment and so enabled it to become the representative frontier denomination. "It is very certain," says Leonard Bacon, "that Wesley himself, with his despotic temper and his High-Church and Tory principles, could not have carried the Methodist movement in the New World onward through the perils of its infancy on the way to so eminent a success as that which was prepared by his vice-regent. Fully possessed of the principles of that autocratic discipline ordained by Wesley, he knew how to use it as not abusing it, being aware that such a discipline can

[173]

continue to subsist, in the long run, only by studying the temper of the subjects of it, and making sure of obedience to orders by making sure that the orders are agreeable, on the whole, to the subjects. More than one polity theoretically aristocratic or monarchic in the atmosphere of our republic has grown into a practically popular government, simply through tact and good judgment in the administration of it, without changing a syllable of its constitution. Very early in the history of the Methodist church it is easy to recognize the aptitude with which Asbury naturalizes himself in the new climate. . . . In spite of the sturdy dictum of Wesley, 'We are not republicans, and do not intend to be,' the salutary and necessary change had already begun which was to accommodate his institutes in practice, and eventually in form, to the habits and requirements of a free people." [14] Not all the credit for this change in the temper of Methodism belongs to Asbury. William McKendree—frontier preacher, presiding elder and, finally, bishop—was largely responsible for the transition from personal absolutism to constitutional government. And the refractory James O'Kelley, who withdrew from the church because of its unwillingness to curb the powers of the bishop, as well as the schism of the Methodist Protestants, who divided from the main body on the issue of lay representation and the election of presiding elders, played an important part in adapting the spirit if not always the constitution of Methodism to the characteristic temper of the West. [15]

With these modifications of its character as a sect of the poor and a child of an aristocratic church, Methodism was able to enter upon an unprecedented career of frontier conquest. It was not entirely unsuccessful elsewhere. In New England it was able to gain some adherents among the poorer classes, profiting there by the revivals, which reflected the greater frontier movement and which Methodism itself promoted. Something of the class character of the Methodists of Massachusetts and Connecticut appears in their relationship to the Jeffersonian Republicans on the one hand and the Federalists on the other. "The great mass, if not the entire, of the Methodist church and her adherents were Republicans," wrote Brunson, the saddle-bag preacher, who was himself a "Yankee," a Methodist, and a Jeffersonian. "Every convert to Methodism, in those times," he goes on to generalize, "became a Republican if he was not one before . . . On the other hand Calvinism and Federalism were yoked together and the dominant *isms* of the state." [16] As in earlier and later times religious denominations, economic classes and political parties showed a considerable amount of correlation in New England. In the South, also, where the Anglican church, as the established church prior to the Revolution, was as neglectful of its mission to the poor as it had been in England and also inefficient in its whole ecclesiastical work,[17] Methodism found a fruitful field for its labors. As Boston was the center of Congregationalism, New York of Episcopalianism, Philadelphia of

Presbyterianism, so Baltimore became the headquarters of early Methodism. In 1779 all but three hundred and nineteen of the 8,577 members reported by the preachers at the annual conference lived south of the Mason and Dixon line; of the 14,988 members reported in 1784 only eleven per cent. resided in the North.[18]

But it was in the country of the new Western democracy which developed after the Revolution—in Kentucky, Tennessee, and Ohio—that Methodism came into its own as the church of the frontier. The camp-meetings, which the Presbyterians had begun but had abandoned when their excesses caused alarm, were taken over enthusiastically by the Methodists, who found this institution as adaptable to their purposes as the watch-night meetings of England had proved to be. With the Baptists the Wesleyans reaped the harvest which McGready and his Presbyterian co-laborers had sown. The rock on which Presbyterianism had split, the licensure or ordination of uneducated but devoted laymen, was a cornerstone of the Methodist system; the Arminian heterodoxy of Presbyterian revivalists was orthodoxy among the followers of Wesley; the emotional demonstrations which Scotch theologians regarded with misgiving, if not with outright revulsion, were evidence of the Holy Spirit's activity for those whose movement had been founded in similar revivals in Bristol and London. Methodism was in tune with the spirit of the frontier to begin with and so it was able to cultivate that spirit wholeheartedly. In one sense the church created the frontier spirit of which, in another sense, it was the child. The result of this accommodation of Methodism to the border was its almost complete victory over the older established churches. The Western conference of the church increased in membership from 2,800 to more than 11,000 during the five years from 1800 to 1805; by 1811 it numbered more than 30,000 members.[19] From Kentucky and Tennessee the missionaries rode south and north and west. Ohio, Indiana and Illinois were visited at the very beginning of their settlement by the tireless circuit-riders and Missouri received its first Methodist missionary as early as 1805.[20] As long as the frontier advanced Methodism kept pace with it. "The Methodist preacher crossed the mountains into Kentucky only ten years behind Daniel Boone, and he gained on Boone's successors. He reached Oregon and California ahead of the first division of the oncoming migration."[21] Although the circuit-rider needed to dispute each frontier with the Baptist missionary, he followed, on the whole, a slightly different course; while the latter evangelized the South and Southwest the former tended to follow the pioneers toward the Northwest. Not only the Carolinas and Georgia, but Mississippi and Louisiana, Missouri, Arkansas, Oklahoma, and Texas were the scenes of Baptist predominance while in the northern belt of states, from Ohio and Michigan to Washington and Oregon the advantage lay with the Methodist. What influence these rival denominations of the frontier exercised in educating the

South to hold fast to its traditional doctrine of local control and the North to espouse the ideal of federalism is a subject for speculation rather than demonstration. The coincidence of the practice of Baptist independency with the ideal of state sovereignty and of the Methodist polity of centralized control with the policy of federal supremacy is striking in any event. Probably interaction between the religious and political tendencies in a common culture took place here as in other cases.

The third great church of the West which took the leadership of the religious life of the nation away from the Eastern denominations during the frontier period was the native-born church of the Disciples of Christ. Methodists and Baptists accommodated themselves to the conditions of the frontier and profited greatly by the harmony of their temper with its spirit; but the Disciples of Christ were a true product of the West. They were the joint result of various frontier movements, beginning with the Republican Methodist revolt of James O'Kelley, the dissolution of the schismatic Springfield presbytery and the subsequent attempt of Marshall and Stone to organize the frontier Christians into an undenominational church, and ending with the attempt of the erstwhile Presbyterian, then Baptist, preacher, Alexander Campbell, to unite all disciples of Christ on the basis of a frontier faith.[22] Like the Baptists and the Methodists, the Disciples used the methods of the revival, fostered immediacy in religious experience through appeal to the emotions, adopted lay preaching, ordained their clergymen without requiring theological education, and organized their churches on the sectarian principle. In all of these respects they represented the frontier spirit. In their effort to overcome the divisions of denominationalism by rejecting creeds and seeking to found a united church on the sole standard of the Bible, they represented a frontier tendency which did not come to expression in the two rival churches. The frontier not only divided its pioneers from the established churches of the East but also impressed upon them a common pattern of religious life and a common religious symbolism. The camp-meeting was an early form of denominational co-operation in which Presbyterian, Methodist and Baptist preachers united. The conversions which took place whether in response to Calvinist preaching or to Arminian appeals were of the same type. The hymns which were sung, the prayers which were offered, the symbols of heaven and hell which were employed, the sins which were condemned and the righteousness which was portrayed, were the hymns, prayers, symbols, sins and virtues of the frontier—not those of any special group. Furthermore, as is the case in almost every migration, adherents of various sects previously isolated were thrown together on the frontier and achieved a social unity which was bound to affect their religious prejudices and divisions.[23] Despite the similarity of their piety Methodists and Baptists could not overcome the inherited differences between their churches, supported as these were by the rivalries of preachers. It remained for an American-born church to express the common character of frontier faith. It was not the common character of the Christian or even of an American version of that religion which was expressed in it. The practices of the churches of established communities, their liturgies, their institutional character, their philosophical defense of the faith, their federal or episcopal organization were scarcely regarded as Christian by the early Disciples; only that interpretation of the New Testament which appeared reasonable from the point of view of the West was regarded as truly Christian. In this instance, as in many other movements of a similar sort, the fact that the New Testament is the book of a first generation of disciples and, therefore, one in which neither the institutional character of a religious community nor the claims of family solidarity could come to very explicit expression was naturally overlooked —much to the advantage of the desired interpretation.

The church of the Disciples remained a Western, but primarily a Middle Western, church. It was not a frontier faith in quite the same way as were Methodism and the Baptist movement. Not only did it start its course later than these, achieving organization only after the frontier had passed hundreds of miles further inland, but it lacked much of the emotional fervour these other denominations possessed. It was somewhat more interested in the social principle of union than in the individual principle of the salvation of souls. Perhaps this was the reason why it was less aggressive than its rivals. It was representative of a West which had passed the storm and stress period of social adolescence and was recovering from its youthful extremities of hope and fear, without having lost the characteristic features the formative years had impressed upon it.

II

The transition from frontier to established society is not without intermediate stages in which the social character of denominationalism again comes to light. The frontier usually passes from the pioneer stage into a period of settled agricultural life. A relatively stable and homogeneous, rural population takes the place of the shifting early settlers. The folkways and modes of an older society reassert themselves; social institutions are established; in the individual life the milder emotions cultivated by ritual take the place of the unstable but extreme experiences of despair and assurance, which the constant crisis of frontier existence called forth; the earlier individualism in government, economics, morality and religion makes way for trust in social institutions and forms. The frontier sect becomes a rural church, in which the sharply defined character, inherited from the pioneer days, has been modified by the influence of social habit. The bright colors are toned down, the mountains and valleys of the spiritual life lose their fearful aspects as their slopes are cultivated and as well-marked highways show the way from depth to height. Now the revival, losing its spontaneous character, becomes a ritual form—a method on which the church and the unredeemed children of converted parents can rely for the desired results. Conversion is regularly expected and occurs with an almost equal regularity. The sectarian organization takes on a churchly aspect, providing means of education in Sunday schools and other agencies, whereby the second and third generations may be instructed in the ways of the fathers. Creeds, whether written or unwritten, become increasingly important as symbols of social unity and social differentiation. Piety remains directed primarily to the salvation of the soul, yet the gain of the less spiritual but none the less desired goods of economic and communal life is also its object.

When the frontier faith becomes domesticated in this way in the rural church, it does not thereby enter into closer relationship with the religion of the older settlements. The latter has in the meantime become urban in character, if it was not so to begin with. Friction between metropolis and farm is substituted for the conflict between established settlement and frontier. The continuance of denominational differences which began amid the difficulties of frontier adjustment is secured not only by the conservatism of social habit but also by the continued divergence of culture. East and West remain divided by the different thought-forms and attitudes nurtured by commercial, metropolitan life and by agricultural economics.

This difference between the former churches of the

frontier and those of the East is illustrated statistically by the proportion of the communicants of each group which reside in the principal cities of the United States. In 1906, before the unusually rapid growth of industry quickened the growth of cities in unprecedented manner, eighty-eight per cent. of all Baptists lived outside of the principal cities; eighty-six per cent. of all Methodists, almost eighty-nine per cent. of the Disciples and ninety-two per cent. of the United Brethren belonged to this class. On the other hand less than fifty per cent. of the communicants of the Protestant Episcopal Church, fifty-four per cent. of the Unitarians, sixty-nine per cent. of the Congregationalists, seventy-two per cent. of the Presbyterians and seventy-five per cent. of the Lutherans were classified in this category.[24] The extent to which this unequal distribution of the communicants of the different denominations affects religious attitudes and forms is not subject to similar accurate measurement. Yet the religious conservatism and theological simplicity, the greater emotional interest, the individualism and continued sectarian organization of the rural churches evidently distinguish them from the urban group. In their espousal of social reforms, also, they reflect the interest of the rural West, whose moral character they largely helped to fashion in the decisive frontier days. They are the supreme champions of prohibition legislation, especially with regard to the use of liquor and to Sabbath observance. The urban and Eastern churches reflect, with variations among them, the more tolerant and more worldly attitudes of a European-born, aristocratic and city-nurtured ethics. These urban churches, however, when they enter the field of social reformation show a larger interest than do the rural churches in the amelioration of industrial conditions. While such generalizations are subject to many individual exceptions—after all, Walter Rauschenbusch was a Baptist—they hold good for the denominations in a broad way.

In recent times the conflict between urban and rural religion took on dramatic form in the theological battles of Modernism and Fundamentalism. The agrarian leader of the West, Bryan, became not only the champion of its economic interests but of its religion also. In the religious position he and his followers represented were reflected not only the memories and habits of frontier faith but also the experiences of rural life. Modernism, however, grew out of the social experience of the city bourgeoisie as well as out of the impact of the new science on religion. Weber has remarked that as the religion of the bourgeoisie tends to center in "practical rationalism in the conduct of life," and in "intra-worldly asceticism," so the religion of the primitive agriculturalist is inclined to magic, to the compulsive spell upon the powers of nature on which the rural worker is so dependent for his whole economic existence. Only very powerful religious revolutions, which have their source in other economic groups or in prophetic personalities, have been able to overcome this native tendency of a primitive peasantry. "Orgiastic and

ecstatic phenomena of possession, induced by intoxi-
cating drugs or by the dance . . . were substituted
among them for the mysticism of the intellectuals." [25]
It is a far cry, to be sure, from the Semitic or Grecian
agricultural religions Weber has in mind to the faith
of the Western, American and Christian farmer. Yet
dependence on the powers ruling nature remains a
constant factor in all agricultural life; the impression
of that dependence is far deeper in the case of the
man who must look to rain and sun for sustenance
than in the case of the industrial worker or of the
business man whose relations to the super-human
forces are obscured, so far as the economic life is concerned, by multitudes of middle-men. This difference is reflected in many of the deeper reaches of the
religious life. Hence the faith of the rural community centers more in the appropriation of the
grace of God that men may live in harmony with
Him, while urban religion is more concerned with
the gain of that same grace that men may live at
peace with one another. Hence also the excesses of
rural religion are found in the realm of magic ideas
and practises while the defects of urban religious
life lie in the field of an unbelieving and impotent
ethics of self-help. To the agriculturalist, furthermore, the symbolism of the Bible, especially of the
Old Testament, is far more familiar through daily
dealing with the phenomena of nature than it can
be to the urban born and bred. And a difference in
symbols often hides a common understanding of
the symbol's meaning, so that those who share a com-

mon faith must quarrel with each other over its expression. Each loses sight of the all-over-arching human fate, of the common human frailty, of the common Divine origin and goal of all human life and striving, and so each demands universal adherence to the standard which appears so reasonable from his perspective.

In more fluid times, with less powerful ecclesiastical organizations in command, the parties of rural Fundamentalism and of bourgeois Modernism might well have produced denominations which would have handed down for many decades in creeds and traditions, the temporary, local differences of opinion found in post-war America. The advantages of strong ecclesiastical organization, in preserving compulsory unity until inner harmony can be re-established, have come to light in this instance as they came much more patently to light in the medieval world.

Rural religion, however, is subject to further transition. The influence of rapid and frequent communication, the increasing dependence of the farm, as of industry, on the human devices of trade and commerce, the extension of urban education to the district schools, the migration of the members of rural denominations to the cities, where they remain loyal to their churches—these and many other influences, which are obvious to everyone, involve the rural churches of the West in a new process of accommodation. Passing through the median stage of agricultural life the churches of the frontier become churches of the city and take on in rapidly increasing measure the character of urban and established culture. Revivalism gives way to education and liturgy; camp-meetings with their high emotions are replaced by Chautauqua assemblies and missionary conferences; the homespun exhortations of the circuit-rider become polished discourses directed to college-bred audiences or screaming perorations addressed to head-line readers; theological seminaries conferring B.D.'s and S.T.M.'s provide successors to the graduates of "Brush College" whose "parchments of literary honor were the horse and the saddle-bags." And spontaneous movements of the spirit among men face to face with strange and vast new problems become the petrified traditions of ecclesiastical organizations—traditions which have often lost significance in a new and common environment but which have not lost their power to keep apart to the third and fourth generations the children of long-forgotten frontiers.

III

The Appalachian Mountains drew the first dividing boundary between American denominations; the Mason and Dixon line bisected the two unequal portions which resulted and added churches of the North and South to the churches of the East and West. In few instances have schisms been so obviously due to the operation of social factors as in the case of the break which the Civil War and its antecedents effected in the churches of America. Rarely have the causes of schism been less obscured by rationalization, for the sister churches of the North and South, whether Presbyterian, or Methodist, or Baptist, or Lutheran continued to confess their creedal unity while maintaining their ecclesiastical separation. Because the social sources of this schism are written so plainly in history it is unnecessary to dwell at length on their description.

One error of popular belief, however, must be guarded against in considering the character of the schism between Northern and Southern Christianity. It is the same fallacy which enters into many discussions of the political divisions. From the point of view of the North the ideal construction which could be put on both separations was to refer them to a difference of moral attitude on the ethical question of slavery. That such a difference was present in the case of individuals and sometimes of groups is not to be denied, but that the divergent judgments on slavery were due, in the main, to any excellence of disinterested moral insight on the part of the North is an untenable rationalization of the true process by which such a social judgment comes to pass. The difference in attitude toward slavery was rooted in a difference of economic interest and structure, of culture and tradition. "The distinctions which characterized the three great sections of the United States evolved in the sweep of economic forces were not fanciful; they were woven out of the tough facts of daily existence," says Beard. "The leaders in all these regions were of the same race, spoke the same language, worshipped the same God, and had a common background of law, ethics and culture. Their differences in sentiments, patterns of thought, and linguistic devices—their social psychology—sprang mainly from divergences in necessary adjustments to environment: labor systems, climate, soil, and natural resources producing conspicuous variations in modes of acquisition and living." [26]

The Northern condemnation of slavery was made possible by the whole economic development of the states north of the Mason and Dixon line, with their small farms and diversified crops, their commercial and industrial interests. The Southern defense of the institution was eventually due to the rising importance of cotton in the world's markets and to the invention of the cotton gin. [27] Prior to the establishment of cotton as king the South had given almost as much voice to the demand for the liberation of slaves as the North. Georgia, at the time of its establishment as a colony, had excluded slavery from its borders and it was the great Evangelical Whitefield who played a large part in introducing it there. [28] In the days of the Revolution the great Virginians— Washington, Jefferson, Henry, Madison, Monroe and John Randolph—condemned it. [29] South Carolina for many years prohibited the importation of slaves. In 1832 the Virginia legislature failed by only one vote to pass a Colonization Act which was intended to accomplish the speedy downfall of the system. [30] Southern preachers and statesmen described slavery as the "heaviest calamity" that has ever been visited upon a nation. On the other hand

[189]

there was much pro-slavery sentiment in the North—notably in Puritan Boston. But the economic forces had their way. Gradually the attitudes of the two sections were consolidated and opposed to each other.

To the economic forces which were primarily responsible for the antagonism and misunderstanding between North and South many other factors, which the histories set forth in detail, must be added. It is necessary to call attention to only one of these in the present connection. The abolition movement was not only a symptom of conflict but one of its causes as well. Unconcerned, frequently, with facts, but swayed by a towering passion for reform, it painted every slave in the guise of an Uncle Tom and every master in the lurid colors of a Simon Legree. In consequence it probably was less effective in influencing the social psychology of the North than in consolidating the pro-slavery feelings of the South. Under the vehement and often unfair attacks of the apostles of reform the South achieved a new sectional solidarity and rallied to the defense of its peculiar institution, which became under the circumstances the symbol of its social loyalties. Once it had been apologetic; the warnings of a bad conscience had manifested themselves in many efforts to discover a reasonable solution of an exceedingly difficult problem. Now, meeting the attack of abolitionism, the South began to find highly moral reasons for the continuation of slavery, and its churches, as a part of the whole Southern culture, were obliged to idealize the peculiar institution.

So the social and psychological differences between South and North came to expression in scriptural condemnations and defenses of slavery. It was plain to Southern Methodists, Baptists, Presbyterians, and Episcopalians that many of the Old Testament heroes they had been taught to venerate had been masters of slaves, that Paul had given his sanction to the institution by counselling obedience to masters and by returning the runaway Onesimus to Philemon.[31] The incompatibility of chattel slavery with the counsel of love was no less evident to the Northern church-goer. The South idealized the patriarchal relations of kindly lords to child-like servants; the North was more aware of the atrocities of domineering slave-drivers and of the brutalities of the slave-market.

The divisions within the denominations which resulted from the increasing division of the two sections did not all follow one pattern. In general it may be said that the sects divided on the slavery issue and the churches divided on the political issue. This is evident from the dates of the various schisms, for while the Baptists and Methodists divided into Northern and Southern branches many years before the outbreak of the Civil War the Presbyterians, Lutherans, and Episcopalians did not separate until secession had taken place.

The attitude of the early Methodists and Baptists toward slavery had been that of men whose own economic and social condition made them sensitive to the sins of inequality and oppression. They were the heirs of a religion of the poor, which had been sympathetic to those elements in the gospel that counselled brotherhood. As sects they had been interested more in the ethics than in the theology of the faith and their rallying point had been a moral conception of Christianity. Furthermore, they had been subjected to the influence of the doctrines of the Revolution much more than the middle-class churches had been, and under the conditions of the frontier their faith in equality and liberty had been effectively nurtured. Hence they had borne testimony against slavery in the beginning of their American career, and especially after the Revolution. The Virginia Association of Baptist churches in 1789 adopted a resolution which declared slavery to be "a violent deprivation of the rights of nature, and inconsistent with a republican government" and recommended to the brethren "to make use of every legal measure to extirpate this horrible evil from the land." [32] The General Conference of the Methodist church in 1780 had acknowledged slavery to be "contrary to the laws of God, man, and nature, and hurtful to society; contrary to the dictates of conscience and pure religion" and passed its disapprobation on all members who kept slaves.[33] Four years later it resolved to expel converts who bought or sold slaves; local preachers who, "in the states where the laws permit it, will not emancipate their slaves," were to be suspended. It elaborated, in the same year, a detailed plan for the extirpation of the "abomination of slavery" and continued, year after year, to bear its testimony against the bondage of the Negro.[34]

But when success attended the missionary efforts of these denominations and when prosperity came to their converts the temptation to relax the vigorous anti-slavery attitude of these early years was inescapable. A historian of the Baptist church writes that the protest against slavery was ineffective and "the great mass of Baptists soon reconciled themselves to the existence of slavery as an institution of the land which they were powerless to abolish, but which they would do everything in their power to mitigate by humane treatment and Christian instruction. Large numbers of slave-owners became Baptists. . . . To free their slaves might have exposed them to worse evils than to retain them under gospel influences. Once recognized as under the circumstances allowable, the large property interest involved was sure, human nature being as it is, to lead Christian slave-owners to seek to justify the institution itself." [35] In the Methodist church similar accommodation to the interests of Southern slaveholders was inevitable. The Methodists of North and South Carolina and Georgia were exempted from the operation of the church rules on the subject.[36] It was ordered that Forms of Discipline be "prepared for the use of the South Carolina Conference, in which the section and rule on slavery be left out." [37] At last, in 1836, the General Conference expressed its opposition to modern abolitionism and disclaimed "any right, wish, or intention, to interfere in the civil and political relation between master and slave as it exists in the slave-holding states of the union." [38] "The sensitive and excited tone of legislation on the subject all through this period [after 1784] indicates that the church had an increasing and considerable number of slave-holders," says the historian of Southern Methodism.[39]

The efforts of Baptists and Methodists to reconcile their traditional position on the subject with the interests of a new well-to-do, slave-holding clientele and to preserve unity between North and South were unavailing. It was inevitable that some sections in each church should be dissatisfied because the attenuated anti-slavery rules or attitudes went too far in condoning slavery and that others should be disappointed because they did not go far enough. The position each sect had reached was one of unstable compromise. They were sects on the way to becoming churches; they could neither maintain the sectarian rule of excluding those who violated the discipline nor the ecclesiastical principle of resigning to the state the decision on all questions involving civil relations. This inner instability coupled with the growing antagonism of the sections made the schism of both churches in 1844 and 1845 inevitable.[40] The issue was an internal one: it involved contrasting attitudes on the part of the two sections of each church on a moral question; the influence of sectionalism, of economic and political factors in defining this moral issue was apparently not comprehended by either side.[41]   Hence there arose the passions of conflict which accompany the strife of those who cannot understand the apparent moral obtuseness of their enemy.   And this conflict engendered habits of thought, prejudices and misunderstandings which played no small rôle in keeping the churches apart after the issue which divided them had been almost forgotten.   The opposite attitudes of the two groups toward the emancipated Negro, which resulted from the ardent passions of the North for equality and of the South for the continued patriarchal supervision of an immature people as well as from the differences between racial relations in a North with few Negroes and in a South with many, were important causes of continued division.   The industrial development of the North after the Civil War and the continued rural character of the South provided for different social developments in the two sections for the space of half a century and during this time the separated churches necessarily followed divergent paths of progress.   Hence the schism which resulted from an issue long adjusted is continued because of differences due to social causes.   With the industrialization of the South, the increase of communication throughout the United States and the slow growth of a homogeneous culture these differences are disappearing.   Yet for the present the churches of North and South, whether Baptist or Methodist, continue to pursue their separate courses.

Presbyterians, Lutherans and Episcopalians also suffered schism as a result of the irrepressible conflict between North and South. In these instances, as has been pointed out, the causes of separation were political rather than moral. The Episcopalian church was divided only during the brief space of the war and its Northern branch refused to consider the separation as anything more than the unavoidable absence of Southern delegates from its conferences. The question of slavery was not involved; even the question of secession was in the background. The presiding bishop of the Northern church published his conviction that secession was a constitutional right of the states and that slavery was sanctioned by the Bible. Though others in the church took an opposite attitude, the passions of conflict were not engendered and ecclesiastical unity was restored almost as soon as political integrity was re-established.[42] The schism of the Lutheran church began when the Southern synods were virtually read out of the General Synod in 1861, not for espousing slavery, but because of the "open sympathy and active co-operation they have given to the cause of treason and insurrection." [43] Unlike the division in the Episcopalian church the Lutheran separation endured for many years, continuing until 1918 when the churches of the North and South reunited in the organization of the United Lutheran Church. The long continuation of the schism in this case was probably partly due to the outspoken support which Northern Lutheranism gave the Federal government and to its severe condemnation of secession. In this attitude it was true to its inherited character as a child of the German state churches. But the continuance of the schism was also caused by differences in the development of the Northern and Southern branches of Lutheranism. The Southern church received fewer additions from Europe both before and after the Civil War than did the Northern branch. Hence it was more quickly Americanized and more strongly influenced by the practices and attitudes of other denominations than was its sister church. The liturgical controversies especially indicate this fact. Reunion was possible in this case when not only the passions of war had been forgotten but when the common adaptation to the American environment brought the two groups again into closer harmony in thought and practice.[44]

In the Presbyterian church, which in constitution and tradition had much in common with the former state churches of Germany and England, the schism between the sectional groups was similarly the result of secession rather than of a slavery controversy. The break came when an ardent anti-abolitionist introduced a resolution in the General Assembly which declared the church's obligation to "promote and perpetuate the integrity of these United States," "to strengthen, uphold and encourage the Federal government" ("as the visible representative of national existence") and which professed "unabated loyalty" to the Constitution.[45] The Southern members of the church, confronted with the choice of declaring loyalty to what was to them an enemy government or of dividing the church, could not escape the necessity of setting up their own establishment. "The whole manner, scope and circumstances of the transaction were purely political," says Thompson,[46] and the Southern church took this position when it affirmed in its first General Assembly that "it is desirable that each nation should contain a separate and independent church." It regarded secession as a decree of Providence, "which in withdrawing their country from the government of the United States, has, at the same time, determined that they should withdraw from the church of their fathers." [47] Under the stress of war both the question of allegiance to the secular government and the problem of slavery became moral issues on which the two branches of the church differed. The Southern church regarded the declaration of the loyalty to the Federal government on the part of the General Assembly as a violation of historic Calvinist and Presbyterian doctrine, a surrender of church to state, and it made the independence of church from the state a major item of its program. Although the first General Assembly of the church in the South had declared that "in our ecclesiastical capacity we are neither the friends nor the foes of slavery; that is to say, we have no commission either to propagate or to abolish it," the Assembly of 1864 hesitated "not to affirm that it is the peculiar mission of the Southern church to conserve the institution of slavery, and to make it a blessing both to master and slave." [48] As in the case of the Methodist and Baptist churches the moral issue which had arisen out of the social situation made the passions of conflict more bitter than they were with Lutherans or Episcopalians. The conflict between the two churches became too severe to allow a speedy reunion after the war and the divergent cultural development of the two sections, together with the different attitudes toward the Negro and the traditional continuation of the defense-mechanisms of conflict, served to prolong the schism decade after decade.

CHAPTER EIGHT

THE CHURCHES OF THE IMMIGRANTS

The immigration of millions of Europeans to the
United States in the eighteenth, nineteenth, and twentieth centuries is one of the major phenomena of
world history, comparable, in a sense, to the tremendous migrations which marked the end of the
ancient world and the beginning of North European
civilization. Not only are its political and economic
effects upon the fortunes of the nations discovered to
be increasingly significant but its importance for religious history is becoming constantly more apparent. In the one case as in the other the result of the
melting of diverse races and cultures remains largely
unrevealed as well as incomplete. Yet significant
tendencies are traceable and some interesting, if partial, results are open to view.

The influence of immigration on politics and economic life in the New World has been conditioned by
the practice of democracy in the one sphere and by
the availability of free land in the other. These
offered a situation in which immigrant groups were
able to develop freely and to assert their specific
character. But they also provided the circumstances which made Americanization possible through
the free incorporation of the new groups in the social

[200]

whole. They prevented the immigrants from becoming political minorities or economic classes, whose self-consciousness as separate groups might have been nurtured by resistance against the coercive measures of a nativistic society.

What democracy and free land have meant for the political and economic development of America the separation of church and state has meant for its religious development. On the one hand that separation has given to each immigrant group the privilege of maintaining and developing its own religious faith; on the other hand it has placed the immigrant churches in an environment of free competition, unprotected and unmolested by state interference, and so it has provided the background for a process of religious accommodation, of a kind of religious Americanization.

The receptivity of America for all sorts of churches has been balanced by the selectivity of emigration. As the American political organization attracted those who were conscious of political oppression in the Old World and desirous of a larger measure of political self-determination; as free land attracted those whose ambition and consciousness of need were sufficiently pronounced to encourage them to overcome the inertia of settled custom and to brave the difficulties of a new orientation; so the freedom of faith drew across the seas many of those who valued religious freedom highly and who smarted under the compulsions of nations bent on enforcing uniformity in worship and belief. The attraction exercised by any one of these factors is often overemphasized. At present it is the fashion to discount as causes of emigration all but the economic motives. The Puritans of Boston and the Lutherans of Missouri, it is maintained, left their native land not because they wanted to gain heaven in their own way but in order that they might win a larger share of an earthly Paradise. Motives are always mixed, and only the omniscience of modern psychology has been able to determine which among many psychic sources of action is decisive. From a more finite point of view it seems idle to deny that the desire for religious freedom, coupled, of course, with desire for free land and for political liberties, has exercised potent attraction on American immigrants from Pilgrims to Doukhobors. This fact has doubtless contributed much to the predominance of sectarian over ecclesiastical Christianity in America, for the sects of Europe have been most often oppressed for their faiths' sake and their membership included those whose economic and political opportunities were scantest. Even in the case of churchmen it is reasonable to suppose that American opportunity attracted those types most whose affection for stability and institutional forms was less pronounced than a venturesome willingness to strike out on new paths. Finally, the tendency of emigration to select the young, who are still adaptable to new situations and modifiable in character, is of importance for the development of immigrant churches and for their departure from the characteristics of the parent establishment.

Two main tendencies may be discerned in the history of the immigrant denominations, constituted in this way of a selected membership and placed in the free, competitive environment of American religious life. The first tendency is toward conformity with the prevalent religious attitudes and practices which have been established by the churches previously acclimated in America. The second tendency is toward the differentiation of the immigrant church from the prevailing type, toward the preservation or development of its distinct character. The tendency toward accommodation and the tendency toward competition interact and are responsible for the rise of new denominations as well as for the merging of immigrant churches.

I

Climate is one of the factors which tend to reduce the religious attitudes and the cultural heritage of immigrants to a common American pattern, but it is difficult to determine the extent and character of its influence. The variability of North American weather conditions, the extremes of heat and cold which succeed each other in the great plains of the West, the consequent stimulation of energy and nervous tension foster an activity which may not be without effect on an activist conception of the religious life.[1] But the tendency toward activism has other, probably more important, sources. Both pioneer life and modern industrialism foster a self-assertive attitude toward the environment. Moreover, the influence of early Puritanism, with its intense promotion of laborious and dutiful living and its activist conception of God, nurtured a social tradition in which work was esteemed as the essential element in life. Hence immigrant churches, though trained in many instances to regard the essence of Christianity as doctrine and the field of the Christian life as contemplation and devotion, have often assumed, under the influence of environment and tradition, that pragmatic attitude toward their faith which characterizes American Christianity. Some churches, because of their heritage, have been more, some less, receptive to this influence of New World activism; but even those which have been most inclined to find salvation in faith alone have needed to make large concessions in their preaching and practice to the doctrine of salvation by or in activity. Such changes of temper are not written into the traditional creeds, but they are revealed in sermons and hymnals and in the organization of ecclesiastical agencies.

The extent to which immigrant churches have adopted a revivalism which was foreign to their original character has been noted in the case of New England Puritans and Southwestern Presbyterians. The Lutherans of the South and Southwest also departed somewhat from their traditional antagonism to all emotionalism and accepted a modicum of the prevalent practices in evangelization. Even Catholicism has been unable to resist the tendency to conform its methods in some degree to the technique of conversion developed by its Protestant rivals. This tendency has been supported by the effort of every immigrant church to keep within its pale the children of the immigrants—the second and third generations, who are prone to conform to the religious as well as to other social customs of the country.

A further modification of the immigrant churches has been made necessary by the American policy of the separation of church and state. Anglicans, Presbyterians, the Reformed Churches, most of the branches of Lutheranism and the Eastern Orthodox Churches enjoyed in Europe the advantages of state support. Their organization was not only modelled on that of the state but was incorporated into the political structure, their financial support was guaranteed by the government, their membership was appointed by its laws, and one of their important functions was the support of the political authorities. Transplanted to the New World such organizations have had reorganization forced upon them, and under the conditions of the new environment such reorganization has tended to follow a common model.

In place of the ecclesiastical principle of a church membership coincident with citizenship these denominations have needed to accept, to some extent at least, the sectarian principle of voluntary membership. Hence they have found it necessary to gain their members by personal appeal—a fact which powerfully reinforced the tendencies toward the acceptance of evangelism and the principle of conversion. At all events the result has been the development of great energy in the work of winning men to the church. Europeans are sometimes astonished that in a country which does not officially recognize church membership and in which no barriers prevent the individual's separation from the church the proportion of avowed Christians to total population should be as high as it is in America. Max Weber has sought for an explanation in the theory that economic sanctions have been substituted for the political sanctions of church adherence.[2] While the theory contains an evident element of truth, a further reason for American loyalty to the church is to be found in the intensive cultivation of that loyalty by the denominations. Without this active program for increasing church membership through evangelism and other means social sanctions alone would scarcely have achieved the result which has been attained. The very lack of any sort of compulsion has placed the responsibility for its maintenance upon the church itself and has invigorated it as no reliance upon political agencies could have done. A further effect of the principle of voluntary membership is the theological movement in immigrant churches, which turns from dogmatism toward mysticism and rationalism. It has been necessary for them to stress personal immediacy in religion, to emphasize the individual appropriation of the gospel in feeling or intellect rather than to rely on social authority. They have found it necessary to foster personal conviction, rather than to depend upon mere assent to the social authority of the creed. Hence they have been tempted on occasion to adopt positivistic interpretations of religion; for it is easier to convince men of the social or economic utility of Christianity than of the truth of its metaphysical and moral content.

The American reorganization of the state churches of Europe has usually required a thorough revision of their fundamental law of government. In their homeland they were ruled by consistories or bishops appointed by the *summus episcopus*, the head of the state (save in the case of the Presbyterian churches). Immigration disestablished them and required the development of some type of polity consonant with the principle of separation of church and state. The general tendency in these churches has been toward the adoption of a democratic, representative form of self-government. This constitution was suggested to them by the long history of Christian councils and synods, by the sectarian or free church principle, and by the political organization of the United States. As the polity of the Roman church followed the pattern of the Roman empire so the American churches incline to organize themselves in conformity with the system of state and national legislatures and executives. Final authority among them is generally vested in a church congress, a general conference, assembly or synod, which legislates for the denomination and chooses its executive officers. Despite many individual variations the adoption of this model of church polity has been so general that a close agreement in the form of ecclesiastical government exists among the Americanized immigrant churches.[3] Coincident with this development of a democratic plan of church government, provision for lay representation in the church councils has generally been made by the denominations. The state churches, which needed to undertake a thorough revision of their polity when they established themselves in America, have sometimes anticipated the sects in making this provision. The general result in this matter also has been the adoption of a relatively uniform policy among the denominations of America.

Finally, the principle of separation of church and state has required the immigrant churches to change their customary attitudes toward the secular government. The national churches were accustomed by tradition and required by law to live in the closest of relationships with the political governments of their states. Their naturalization in America required them not only to forswear their old allegiance but also to define their attitude toward the government of the new country in terms compatible with the principle of separation of church and state. The process whereby the Protestant Episcopal Church was divorced from its traditional association with the English crown and adjusted to the situation created by the Revolution is an outstanding example of this type of modification. The difficulty of that change can be well understood if it is remembered that in addition to the legal bonds which united the established church with the government of the colonies a very strong social bond, a tradition of loyalty to the king, had been forged during the years of the English

Civil War, Commonwealth, Restoration and Revolution. During that century of strife in England the support of the crown had become almost a chief requirement of orthodoxy in the established church. As the English state church in revolting English colonies Anglicanism probably faced one of the most difficult problems a major religious organization has had to deal with in America. That it should remain Royalist throughout the Revolution was most natural; but that when the separation of the colonies from the homeland had been accomplished the church should be able to slough off the tradition of centuries and should become able to reorganize itself as an American Episcopalianism is one of the most admirable facts in the church history of the United States. In renouncing its older political allegiance Episcopalianism effectively eliminated from its organism that political character which had become one of its chief marks. In its Book of Common Prayer it substituted the President and Congress for the King, but it eliminated English royalty from its affections without the substitution of an equal political symbol. It became a church which "hath ever renounced all political association and action" and mingled less in the strife of parties than any other denomination with national membership. Hence it passed through the American Civil War with little loss; and even when its homeland was involved in the titanic struggle of the Great War it cultivated an aloofness from political interests which set it in marked contrast to many sects.[4]

The history of other national churches has been similar in many respects to the history of the English church. In general it may be said that the political churches of the Old World have become less political in the New World than have the non-political sects of Europe. While they have cast off their old political loyalties they have retained a strong sense of the authority of the "powers ordained of God." They have carried over into their new environment the attitude of acceptance of constituted rule which their past history had written deeply into their character. Partly because of their unfamiliarity and lack of sympathy with the processes of democracy but more because of their traditional philosophy of acceptance they have refrained from attempts to interfere with the legislative functions of the state. Exceptions to this rule have occurred when their own ecclesiastical interests were directly attacked, as in the case of parochial schools and church colleges. But on the whole the American principle of the separation of church and state has been more effectively represented by the churches which were once the organs of the state than by the sects which rose in revolt against state dominance of religion. When the supremacy of the state over all other interests has been asserted, as in times of war, the churches have yielded to the political interests on the ground that they owed obedience to secular authorities. The sects, on the other hand, though they have identified themselves no less readily with the state under these circumstances have usually done so by idealizing

the cause of the state and by christening the war a
Holy War. Thus, as has been pointed out, the
churches were divided in the days of the Civil War
by the secession issue, but the sects by the slavery
issue. The latter supported the conflict as a crusade
against vice, while the former simply expressed their
loyalty to the constituted governments. Similar differences between churches and sects marked the en-
trance of the United States into the World War, although by that time the churches had become somewhat more sectarian in their attitudes.

So the accommodation of the immigrant churches
to the new political environment has tended in some
respects toward the establishment of a new, common
American church type. In polity, in lay representation, in the adoption of the principle of voluntary
membership, in common abstention from interference
in the processes of civil government, the immigrant
national churches have approached a common form.
This tendency toward uniformity has been reinforced
by their common assimilation of a new culture as
well as by their common adjustment to a new type
of civil government.

One of the most important elements in culture is
language and every European church in America,
save those whose native tongue was English, has been
required to make its accommodation to this factor.
The language question has been one of the most difficult problems with which the immigrant churches
have had to deal, for it involved the problem of rebirth in a new civilization. Conservatives in these

churches have always maintained that the abandonment of the old, European tongue and the adoption
of English as the language of worship and instruction involved the abandonment of all the ways of the
fathers and the introduction of a new "English or
American religion." Their intuitions have usually
been correct, for the adoption of the native tongue
is only the most obvious symptom of the assimilation
of the native culture as a whole. Progressive, that
is more Americanized, leaders have argued for two
centuries in immigrant church after immigrant
church that the abandonment of the foreign language
was essential for the self-preservation of the denomination concerned. Their reasoning has also been
sound, for it is a well-known fact that institutions are
much more conservative than individuals and that
churches will continue to pray, preach and teach in
Dutch or German or Swedish long after the major
number of their members have dropped these languages in all save religious relations and have raised
a generation of children to whom the mother tongue
is a foreign sound. The choice between accommodation and extinction finally becomes a forced choice.
Though churches may delay the moment of their surrender few elect to perish with their mother tongue.
With the adoption of English as the church language
other changes inevitably set in. The poetry of worship in liturgies and hymns is essentially untrans-
latable. Though the immigrant church may make
valiant efforts to retain its old forms within the medium of the new language, though it may succeed in

holding fast to such classics as "Holy Night" and "A Mighty Fortress Is Our God," yet the charm has departed from prayers, songs and litanies which some uninspired poetaster has turned into a conglomerate of English words. More gracious, native, English forms gradually take the place of these compromises between the new and the old, and the worship of immigrant churches is conformed in pattern to that of previously established denominations. What is true of worship is true of instruction, of the methods of evangelism, and eventually, of creeds, confessions of faith, and the general conceptions of the Christian life. The change of language is only one aspect of adjustment to the total culture with its democratic spirit, its industrialism, its patriotism. The process of accommodation as a whole gradually transforms the churches of the immigrants into American denominations with marked similarities and with remarkable dissimilarities from the parent churches of Europe.

II

The tendency toward conformity with the new civilization is, strangely enough, responsible for much of the denominationalism of America. It separates various generations of immigrants from each other so effectively that new schisms result. The members of a European church coming to the New World after their church has been established on American soil for some time frequently find themselves ill at ease among their partly Americanized kindred and feel compelled to organize new denominations which will be truer to the Old World customs. The accommodation of the older immigrant group to the new civilization, the adoption of the native language and of native forms of church life, the rise also of this older immigration in economic position, make the two generations of immigrants essentially alien to each other. Changes in the European church during the period between the two immigrations contribute also to this separation of the earlier and later groups. Thus at about the time when the Dutch Reformed Church became the Reformed Church in America the True Dutch Reformed Church was organized by the newer immigration from the Netherlands. These churches were in agreement in their acceptance of the old Dutch creeds; the explicit issue between them was the use of hymns or psalms in worship, for the Reformed Church in America had given up the ancient custom of singing psalms and adopted the hymnody of other American churches. The implicit issues included the whole subject of adaptation or resistance to the native culture. The process of Americanization, however, did not leave the True Dutch Reformed Church untouched. In the course of time all reference to the European background of the church has been dropped from its title; it became The Christian Reformed Church. By such changes of name a great many internal changes are implied.[5]

Differences in degree of accommodation have played an important part in the atomization of German Lutheranism, though many other factors were also at work to secure this result. One of the marked differences between the Northern and Southern branches of the old General Synod of the Lutheran church, as has been pointed out, was the greater adjustment of the Southern group to American church methods and forms—a fact largely due to the influx of German immigration into the North after the Civil War. Again the division of the old General Council of the Evangelical Lutheran Church from the General Synod, though officially and externally due to doctrinal dissension, was in no small part caused by the conservatism of a later generation of immigrants and of those Pennsylvania Lutherans who had isolated themselves most successfully from the main currents of American life and so had been able to retain their original character most faithfully. Still further to the west and representative of a later immigration than the General Council the Synodical or Missouri conference was organized as a fourth independent branch of German Lutheranism. Its conservative theological character was in part due to the religious situation which this group of immigrants faced in Germany, especially in Saxony, before their migration, in part it was due to the strong leadership of the ultra-conservative Walther, but differences in assimilation of American culture between this Western and most recent group and the earlier Eastern groups of immigrants also played a rôle in keeping these sections of German Lutheranism apart. The establishment in Missouri and Illinois

[215]

of the German Evangelical Synod, independent of the older German groups in the East, involved similar factors. Its marked difference from the conservative Lutheran churches of the West was due to a difference in European background; its difference from the Lutheran churches of the East was due to the differences between generations of immigrants.[6]

In the establishment of various Danish, Norwegian and Swedish churches similar factors seem to have been operative. Two facts, however, have prevented the dismemberment of Scandinavian Christianity in a way comparable to that which prevails in German Lutheranism. In the first place Sweden, Norway and Denmark have enjoyed national existence for a longer period than Germany and their populations have been religiously and culturally more homogeneous than were those of provincialized Central Europe prior to 1870. Historically, also, there have been no such cultural revolutions in the history of these northern countries since immigration to America began, as were caused in Germany by Napoleon and Bismarck. In the second place, the process of accommodation to American civilization has been more rapid and more even among the Scandinavians than among the Germans. Scandinavian immigration to America was practically confined to the fifty years between the close of the Civil War and the outbreak of the World War; hence the differences between early and late arrivals in America have not been so pronounced as in the case of eighteenth- and nineteenth-century German immigrations, and Amer-

icanization has proceeded more evenly. Furthermore, it is a well established fact that the Scandinavians have accepted the English language and
American customs much more readily than did their
German kinsmen.[7] The result of these factors appears in the presence in America of a united Norwegian Lutheran Church, formed in 1917 after union
enterprises had been fostered for a generation, and in
the virtual monopoly of Swedish Lutheranism by the
Augustana Synod.

Yet Scandinavian Lutheranism has not been without its schisms. The process of accommodation to
the new and common environment has not gone so
far that union between the closely allied churches
of the three nations, not to speak of union with the
German churches, has been found practicable. Practical uniformity in matters of creed between these
various groups—they all subscribe to the Augsburg
Confession at least—has not sufficed to bring organic
union. Repeated attempts to unite the Germans and
Swedish or Norwegian and Danish Lutherans have
failed. Furthermore, there has been a tendency in
the free atmosphere of America for parties which a
state church held together to organize as separate
denominations. This tendency is illustrated by the
history of Norwegian Lutheranism prior to the union
of 1917, and by the continuation of two major
Danish Lutheran churches. In these instances an incomplete adjustment to American conditions—the
acceptance of the principle of freedom and the retention of Old World differences—has led to schism.[8]

The process of accommodation may finally be illustrated by reference to a group of English-speaking churches of which fewer adjustments were required by the new environment than was the case with the foreign-language groups. The Scotch Covenanters and Seceders, who arrived in the colonies before the Revolution, were divided from each other by their different attitudes toward the civil government. When these differences were removed or made archaic by the separation of church and state in America, the two groups proceeded to unite in the Associate Reformed Church. This union, however, was recognized neither by the Scotch parent bodies nor by newly arrived or isolated immigrants from the Old World.[9] The result was the continuation of three distinct groups, the Reformed Presbytery, the Associate Presbytery and united Associate Reformed Church. Similarly the effort to unite the Burgher and Anti-Burgher factions of the Seceder church came to grief on the rock of Old World opposition despite the fact that the historic differences between the two groups had no significance in the new America.[10] The difficulty of adjusting forms and ideals fashioned in Scotland to the new American situation and of reconciling the interest of various generations of immigrants resulted in a number of schisms in these Presbyterian churches. The Reformed Dissenting Presbytery withdrew from the Associate Reformed Church; the Reformed Presbytery divided into conservative and progressive branches and the former of these branches again suffered schism with the organization of the Reformed Presbytery of North America.[11] Characteristically, the questions which were most frequently at issue between the conflicting groups were questions of the relationship of the church to the civil government, of the use of psalms or hymns, and of the attitude of the church toward secret societies. At the same time varying degrees of adjustment to the American scene were responsible for those schisms in the main body of Presbyterianism, which have been described in connection with the story of frontier Christianity. The first effect, then, of combining Old World differences with American religious freedom and with the social differences of the New World was—among the Scotch as among the Germans—the multiplication of churches.

But accommodation proceeded until union was possible. Immigration from Scotland and Ulster fell off. National self-consciousness increased greatly in the period between the Revolution and 1812 and Americanization went on apace. The Civil War and its antecedents contributed much to the breaking down of barriers between isolated groups in the North and South by nurturing a common sectional consciousness. The United Presbyterian church succeeded in amalgamating in 1858 the larger groups of Covenanters and Seceders; Old and New Side Presbyterianism merged in the South during the war and in the North shortly after the conclusion of peace. Under the stress of war and reconstruction other union movements flourished; the Southern church absorbed not less than seven independent Presbyterian groups between 1863 and 1874.[12] Only isolation enabled some small remnants of Covenanter and Seceder Presbyterianism to maintain themselves in independence from the united body, though the hoary traditions of seventeenth- and eighteenth-century conflicts in Scotland, to which they appealed for justification of their separate existence, had lost meaning in nineteenth-century America.

So the Americanization of the immigrant churches has gone on. Adapting themselves to a common mould they have grown very much like each other and have made notable progress toward the foundation of that American Christianity which will inevitably appear when the melting pot has completed its synthetic work.

III

The process whereby the immigrant churches have been adapted to a common environment has not been a simple one. It has met many obstacles, and synthesis has been delayed by many opposing forces. Alongside of the factors which made for accommodation other factors which brought forth competition have been present in this as in every other social complex. The process of synthesis has been accompanied by differentiation. The churches of the immigrants have grown like each other in some respects, but in other respects they have tended to differentiate themselves and to emphasize their unique individualities. They were transplanted into a common social environment but at the same time they were set into the midst of a competitive system of denominationalism. The separation of church and state provided the

conditions not only for free assimilation of the culture
and so for synthesis, but also for conflict with other
religious organizations and so for diversity. It was
necessary for many churches which had enjoyed a
virtual monopoly in their European homeland to
compete actively for the loyalty of their members and
for their position in the new society. The situation,
as is the case in other kinds of competition, promoted
a high social self-consciousness and the emphasis of
the peculiar characteristics of the group. Agreements with competitors were minimized, disagreements stressed.

The influence of competition, however, was not
confined to this rivalry with other sects. The
churches of the immigrants were involved in the whole
complex pattern of conflict between the native and
the "foreign" groups. The economic, cultural and
political phases of this conflict were reflected again
and again in religious rivalry and in the religious
self-assertion of the immigrants. The cross-currents
of such social interaction are illustrated today by the
relations of Jews and Gentiles, and, especially, of
Catholics and Protestants. In many of the cities
of America the opposition of a Protestant, Nordic,
middle-class party to a Catholic, south-European,
proletarian group is the basis of political battles; and
the political cleavage in turn reinforces the religious
conflict.[13]

In an earlier era the conflict between the native
population and Dutch, Irish, German, and Scandinavian immigrants had similar economic, cultural, and

political aspects. And it profoundly influenced the denominationalism of the immigrants by involving their religious life in the whole pattern of competition. The suspicion with which the indigenous population regarded early German and Irish immigrants had economic sources, in part, for the immigrant has ever been a threat to the native standard of living.[14] It had cultural aspects as well. The newcomers were mostly poor, they were often illiterate, sometimes thriftless, always different in their language and customs. The sense of superiority which every native possesses had many opportunities for growth and many occasions for expression. Under the circumstances the development of hostility was natural, as it was later when Italians and Slavs supplanted Germans and Irish in the steerages of trans-Atlantic ships. Hostility called forth hostility; the assertion of superiority by one group called forth corresponding self-assertion in the other and the whole situation of conflict issued in a sense of racial or cultural solidarity within each of the antagonistic societies. As a result of this social process the immigrants tended to become a distinct social class with a highly developed self-consciousness. They attended now to the values which the new environment threatened—to their language and their traditions. These were both the uniting bonds of the group and the symbols of its social solidarity. It was necessary, too, for the immigrants under these circumstances to find a center around which they could organize their values, a leadership which would hold together the scattered individuals of the race, a form of organization which would enable them to maintain and foster their solidarity. The only center which was available, as a rule, was religion; the only leaders, with few exceptions, who had braved the difficulties of a new orientation along with the migrating artisans and farmers were the clergy; the only organization which was readily at hand for maintaining the unity of the group was the church. Of literary culture the average immigrant had little. Neither Goethe nor Nietzsche was more than a name to him, but Luther and the German Bible or the crucifix and the mass he knew. These then became symbols of that whole past to which distance, the trials of the New World, and the exigencies of conflict lent a new enchantment. The preacher or priest, moreover, was often the only educated man in the immigrant community. To him the old culture was not merely a mass of memories but a literature and an art expressive of a national genius. He expressed for his countrymen their inarticulate loyalties and fostered their sense for these cultural values. The church with its use of the old language, with its conservative continuance of Old World customs, with its strictly racial character was the most important of the social organizations of the immigrant.

In this way many an immigrant church became more a racial and cultural than a religious institution in the New World. Its parochial schools were fostered not only that the children might receive instruction in religion but also that they might learn the mother-tongue and with it the attitudes and social ideals of the old homeland. In many a Sunday School German or Swedish readers were the only text-books; in many a pulpit the duty of loyalty to the old language was almost as frequent a theme as the duty of loyalty to the old faith. So the churches of the immigrants often found a new and additional reason for their separate existence. They now represented racial sectarianism as in the land of their birth they had represented the principle of ecclesiastical uniformity. They became competitive conflict societies, intent upon maintaining their distinction from other groups, no matter how closely these might be akin to them in doctrine, polity and piety.

The cultural or racial character of such sectarianism usually comes to light when the accommodation of a part of the immigrant population to the new civilization has proceeded so far that the language question arises. An early and interesting example of the common situation is offered by the story of a language controversy in the Dutch Reformed Church of New York in the middle of the eighteenth century. William Livingstone, one of the earliest English preachers in that church, wrote in 1754 that "to prevent the ruin of the Dutch churches common sense pointed out the absolute necessity of disuniting them from the language by translating the public Acts of devotion and worship into English." The suggestion aroused a storm of protest. "Recourse was had" by the anti-English party "to their old practice of reviling and calumniating the Presby-

terians, who were charged with a design no less wicked
than false and impossible, of seizing the Dutch
churches and converting them and their congregations to their own use." "Who cannot see," said Livingstone, "that the grand design was to prevent the
introduction of the English tongue into the Dutch
churches lest the discriminating badge with the vulgar, the difference of language, being removed, a
coalition might ensue and Presbyterianism by that
means be strengthened and supported, while the aug-
mentation of the English by proselytes from the
Dutch Church would in a great degree be inter-
rupted . . . The truth is that those who oppose the
introduction of the English tongue into one of the
Dutch churches are convinced that the different
languages are the only criteria to distinguish them
from each other, and this is evident from their fear
that the use of the same tongue will naturally produce an union. Yet surely it cannot be so destructive
of the interests of the Dutch churches to coalesce with
a sect with whom they perfectly agree in doctrine,
worship and government." [15] In this instance the
Dutch church sought to maintain its language
largely, it seems, as symbol of prestige, which pro-
tected its membership from too intimate an association with the newly arrived "vulgar" Scotch-Irish.
But in this as in many other instances the instinct of
self-preservation was also clearly operative. Without the Dutch language the church, it appeared to
many of its members, would lose its reason for existence since confessionally it was very similar to the

Scotch Presbyterian and German Reformed churches, the representatives of which in the United States far outnumbered the Dutch.

Examples of language controversies in which a racially sectarian consciousness nurtured by competition came to expression may be found in the history of most other immigrant churches in the United States. The experiences of the German Lutheran and German Reformed churches are enlightening on this point. After the American Revolution a strong tendency toward conformity with the social environment set in among their American-born members. The Germans became aware of the danger that threatened their language and culture and they responded with a new insistence upon the retention of the German tongue in their churches. In a liturgy adopted by the Lutheran churches in Pennsylvania in 1786 the following passage occurs in a general prayer ordained for use every Sunday morning: "And since it has pleased Thee, by means of the Germans, to transform this state into a blooming garden, and the desert into a pleasant pasturage, help us not to deny our nation, but to endeavor that our youth may be so educated that German schools and churches may not only be sustained, but may attain a still more flourishing condition." [16] In 1805 the Lutheran Ministerium of Philadelphia passed a resolution which provided that it must remain a German speaking ministerium and which forbade the introduction of any measure "which would necessitate the use of any other language than the German in syn-

odical sessions." [17] The German and English parties
came into conflict in many local churches and frequently divided into two separate congregations.
At the same time dreams of the establishment of a
German culture in America were fostered by conflict with the English and Scotch-Irish settlers and by
the literary renaissance of the homeland. "The English and the German cannot work together. The one
says Shibboleth, the other Sibboleth," wrote a cor-
respondent in a German paper in Pennsylvania and
this was a general feeling among Pennsylvania Germans who felt their racial solidarity threatened by
the defection of youth to American ways and to the
English language. The alternative to accommodation was glowingly set forth by a writer in a Lutheran
magazine in 1813. "What would Philadelphia be
in forty years if the Germans there were to remain
German, and retain their language and customs?" he
asked. "It would not be forty years until Philadelphia would be a German city, just as York and Lan-
caster are German counties. . . . What would be the
result throughout Pennsylvania and Maryland in
forty or fifty years? An entirely German state,
where, as formerly in Germantown, the beautiful
German language would be used in the legislative
halls and the courts of justice." [18] Similar hopes
were to be voiced a generation later in the Middle
West, in Missouri, Illinois and Wisconsin.

The German Reformed Church was involved in the
same conflict. It allowed its great leader, Michael
Schlatter, to retire under a cloud because he was

suspected of having fostered the Anglicization of
Pennsylvania Germans through his interest in charity
schools.[19] It entered into very close relationships
with the German Lutherans, although its religious
and doctrinal affiliations were with the Dutch Reformed Church and with Scotch Presbyterians and
although it had derived its chief financial support for
many years from the national church of the Netherlands. The racial consciousness was stronger than
the denominational. Hence the German Reformed
church undertook to establish, in co-operation with
the Lutherans, a German college and both groups
entertained the thought of organic union with each
other. The school, it is worth noting, was threatened
with extinction when the remarks of an English-
speaking member of the faculty convinced many supporters that it was to become simply another means
toward their Anglicization.[20] It was a time "when language became the watchword which awakened greater
zeal than that of faith," [21] and doctrinal distinctions
between culturally similar churches counted for nothing. Union between German Lutheran and German
Reformed Churches did not come to pass because the
bond of union effective in this period became more
and more tenuous as the process of accommodation
to the American environment continued. At the same
time attempts to consummate the union brought to
light doctrinal differences which the common conflict with the English-speaking churches had obscured. These doctrinal differences, furthermore, received a new emphasis as the competitive organiza-

tions needed to give up their old claims on racial loyalty and to substitute for them new claims based on other reasons for the allegiance of their members.

The histories of most other foreign-language immigrant churches repeat these conflicts between the language parties in the church, the emphasis on the cultural character of the religious organization, the effort to foster through the church the old customs and ideals as well as the racial tongue, and also the gradual acceptance by the immigrants of the language and the modes of the new environment. During the first period of competition and of economic conflict between immigrants and natives the churches of the immigrants tend to differentiate themselves as cultural organizations, which maintain and emphasize their separate individuality not on doctrinal but on cultural grounds. But after accommodation has set in, after the old language and the old ways have been irretrievably lost, after contacts with native churches have increased, the battle ground of competition changes. Ecclesiastical and doctrinal issues replace the cultural lines of division, and the loyalty of an English-speaking, second generation is fostered by appeal to different motives than were found effective among the immigrants themselves. The need for continued differentiation and for the self-justification of an organism which is strongly desirous of continuing its existence, are responsible now for a new emphasis. Denominational separateness in a competitive situation finds its justification under these circumstances in the accentuation of the theological or liturgical peculiarities of the group. Resistance to assimilation continues, but the immigrant church in its battle with other sects for membership and position takes up a new strategic position.

The influence of competition on doctrinal differentiation is, of course, not confined to the foreign-language churches. Whenever rivalry has arisen between culturally similar groups the doctrinal strategy has usually been adopted. As has been pointed out in another connection, competition with Arminian Methodists was largely responsible for the change of doctrine in the Baptist Church from Arminianism to Calvinism.[22] The effect of competition on the Episcopal church was similar in some respects. As Leonard Bacon has said, this church, at the beginning of the nineteenth century, seemed "to have very little to contribute by way of enriching the diversity of American sects." Apart from its "ritual of worship and its traditions of order and decorum," "it simply appeared as the feeblest of the communions bearing the common family traits of the Great Awakening." [23] It was losing members constantly to Methodists, Presbyterians and Congregationalists. Its own tendency toward an ever greater accommodation to the prevailing type of religious life in America failed to stop this loss of members. Under the leadership of Bishop Hobart, however, it executed a *volte-face*. From adjustment it turned to competition; from emphasis upon its essential similarity to other churches it turned to the accentuation of its peculiar character. The principles which Hobart stressed were not those of accommodation but those of differentiation: "The church (meaning his own fragment of the church) the one channel of saving grace; the vehicles of that grace, the sacraments, valid only when ministered by a priesthood with the right pedigree of ordination; submission to the constituted authorities of the church absolutely unlimited, except by clear divine requirements; abstinence from prayer-meetings; firm opposition to revivals of religion; refusal of co-operation with Christians outside of his own sect in endeavors for the general advancement of religion." [24] This program and the effects of the Tractarian controversy plunged the Episcopal church into an internal conflict between the parties of accommodation and of ecclesiastical self-assertion. The latter achieved the victory and the Episcopal church took its place among the competing sects as a very distinctive organization.[25] "Its time of apology was past. It might be liked or disliked, opposed or favored; but it was henceforth recognized as an organization with distinct claims of its own, and with a distinct determination to prosecute them. It stood no longer on the defensive. It became self-conscious, self-confident and self-assertive." [26] While one man furnished the leadership in this process it was the total competitive situation which gave him his opportunity and made his measures effective.

A tendency of a very similar sort was inaugurated in the Lutheran church in the Eastern states at about the same time. It has often been considered an anomalous fact that the Lutheran churches of America should be so much more conservative in their doctrine than are the Lutheran churches of Germany from which they took their rise. Yet the fact is not strange when it is considered that in Germany and Scandinavia these churches enjoyed a virtual monopoly while in America they were placed in competition with hundreds of rival sects. Lutheranism in defense of its continued existence as a church in the United States was forced back upon its doctrinal standards after the early period of cultural competition had passed. During the latter part of the eighteenth century and the early part of the nineteenth there was a strong tendency in American Lutheranism toward assimilation of the prevailing type of religious life and practice as well as of the prevailing culture. Pietistic influences inclined many of the German preachers and settlers to accept or to imitate the methods of the Methodist revival and the Great Awakening. Lutheranism cultivated relations with the Church of England and its leaders considered the possibility of organic union with this church. Its great leader, Muhlenberg, was not very conscious of denominational lines.[27] Toward the close of the eighteenth century, when the tendency toward accommodation was at its height, the two largest Lutheran bodies in the New World, the Ministeriums of New York and of Pennsylvania, adopted new constitutions from which "all reference either to the Augsburg Confession or to the other symbolical books had vanished." [28] Schemes for the organic union of the Lutheran and Reformed churches were favored by many ministers. But the accommodation of both churches to the American environment, their common acceptance of the English language especially, dissolved the tie that had bound them together as allies in the struggle for the preservation of their German culture. They became rivals rather than allies and were placed into competition at the same time with the other churches. As a result of the situation both groups achieved a centralized denominational organization, and denominational self-consciousness was nurtured in consequence. But a more important result of the competition into which the Lutheran church was placed by its increasing adoption of the English language was the assertion of its doctrinal peculiarities. "The General Synod," a historian of the Lutheran church writes, "was a protest against the Socinianizing tendency in New York and the schemes of union with the Reformed in Pennsylvania and with the Episcopalians in North Carolina. It stood for the independent existence of the Lutheran Church in America, and the clear and unequivocal expression of a positive," that is, a Lutheran, "faith." "The General Synod saved the church, as it became Anglicized, from the calamity of the type of doctrine which within the New York Ministerium had been introduced into the English language." [29] Later attempts to bring the church into closer relation with other American denominations, such as those promoted by the Lutheran theologian Schmucker, resulted in a reaction toward ever more conservative Lutheran doctrinal positions.[30] The tendency continued throughout the years until today the United Lutheran Church represents a far more conservative Lutheran position in doctrine than did its ecclesiastical forebears in the early nineteenth century. Lutheranism in the Western states has followed this conservative tendency to an even greater degree. As in the case of the Episcopal church the return to doctrinal and liturgical uniqueness was influenced by European movements. The reaction against the union in Germany of the Reformed and Lutheran churches had something of the same effect on Lutheranism that the Tractarian movement had on Episcopalianism. But in both instances the competitive situation in American church life conditioned the acceptance and reinforcement of conservative influences from the old homeland.

Competition has affected in comparable manner almost all of the churches of America. During the expansive period in American life between 1812 and the Civil War denominational self-assertion, nurtured by conflict on the frontier and among the hosts of newly arriving immigrants, grew apace. Doctrinal controversy filled the air. Each sect was prone to urge its claims as the sole avenue to salvation. And within each denomination the parties of accommodation and of self-assertion fought endless battles. The church seemed to accept a religious version of the doctrine of *laissez faire* and the belief that enlightened self-interest was the agent of divine providence.

The intellectual and religious climate which accompanied these doctrinal storms lay heavy on the land until well into the twentieth century. But competition, as in other relations, tended to pass over into co-operation. It fostered contact and so a measure of understanding between the rival groups. Political and social developments, at the same time, overcame the racial and sectional provincialisms which had divided the religious organizations. The increase of irreligion centered the attention of struggling churches on a common enemy and bade them ally for the sake of self-defense. So accommodation and synthesis seemed to be on the way to victory over competition and differentiation.

CHAPTER NINE

DENOMINATIONALISM AND THE COLOR LINE

The social causes of schism have been obscured so frequently by theological rationalization that the frankness with which the color line has been drawn in the church is unusual. No partisan maintains that the Colored Methodist Episcopal Church and the Methodist Episcopal Church, South, were divided from each other by heresy or that the separation of the colored from the white Baptists was occasioned by doctrinal disputes. In view of the similarity of the theology, ritual and organization of the separated groups any attempt at theological rationalization of the differences between them would probably have been vain. The lack of theological speculation among the Negroes may also have been responsible for the absence of efforts to interpret schism in religious terms. But, on the whole, the sufficient reason for the frankness with which the color line has been drawn in the church is the fact that race discrimination is so respectable an attitude in America that it could be accepted by the church without subterfuge of any sort.

Rationalization has been used to defend discrimination rather than to obscure it. The dogma which divides the racial churches is anthropological, not theological, in content. Whether the dogma of white superiority and Negro inferiority has been openly avowed or unconsciously accepted, the white churches have nevertheless taken it for granted and have come to regard it as not incompatible with the remainder of their beliefs. At times, indeed, they have incorporated it in their popular theology and sought to provide a biblical basis for it, usually by means of a mythological interpretation of the curse of Ham and a corresponding mythological anthropology. More frequently they have received it as a simple dogma of nature, similar to the doctrine of sex. In both cases the assumption of superiority by one group —an assumption which became unquestioned social tradition—has been given the dignity of an impartial natural law and regarded as a self-evident truth. By virtue of the marvellous inconsistency of human reason, it has often been maintained unchallenged alongside of the other self-evident truth that all men are created free and equal and endowed with the same rights to life, liberty, and the pursuit of happiness. Just as the church accepted the doctrine of female inferiority and refused women the right to be ordained or even to participate in its government, so also it accepted the dogma of Negro inferiority and without compunction refused ecclesiastical equality to this race. As it separated men and women in the houses of worship so it segregated and continues to segregate the races. The fact that in Christ there is neither male nor female has, of course, been recognized much more freely in the church than has the fact that in him there can be neither white

[237]

nor black. Even the truth that in him there is neither bond nor free has been more definitely accepted than the implied doctrine of racial equality and unity. Perhaps this difference in the acceptance of various phases of Jesus' and Paul's ideal is due to the universality of the one type of relationship and to the less frequent occurrence of the other type. The church could not escape the duty of dealing with the relationships of men and women and of masters and slaves. But races can be isolated from each other and the race problem can be ignored. After the close association of Jews and Gentiles in early Christianity had ceased, the question of race relations in the church of Christ did not emerge again as a challenging problem until modern times. It was possible for Christians to regard Paul's statement, that in Christ there is neither Jew nor Greek, from a purely historical point of view without endeavoring to apply the principle involved; it was not possible to deal with the relations of the sexes and of masters and slaves in the church in the same way. On the whole, however, the ideal of unity and equality has never been recognized in reality until the inferior group, whether women or slaves or a racial group, has asserted that equality and compelled the church to translate its principles into practice.

It is true that the church has had its seasons of enthusiasm for brotherhood and courageous leaders, who sought to apply the ethics of the gospel to the relations of the races. But the latter frequently suffered an early disillusionment when confronted with the stubborn obstacles of race prejudice and social custom. The days of enthusiasm passed away and the church compromised its principle of brotherhood by dividing into white and black groups, as previously it had compromised by dividing into religious societies of the rich and poor and of the nations. The racial schism is primarily a phenomenon of American religious life, but the color problem is not solely American. The rise of missionary churches in Asia and Africa has made it a world problem. The schisms of the future, it may be, are more likely to be racial schisms than economic or even national divisions of the church.

I

The existence of the racial schism in America is one of the clearest facts in the whole mixed pattern of American denominationalism. Four great denominations, the National Baptist Convention, the African Methodist Episcopal, the African Methodist Episcopal Zion and the Colored Methodist Episcopal churches are purely Negro organizations. In addition to these major organizations there are in the United States a score of smaller all-Negro groups. These Negro denominations have a membership of more than four and a half million. In contrast, less than six hundred and fifty thousand Negro Christians are members of churches of a mixed racial character. Nearly ninety per cent. of all Negro Christians, therefore, are members of churches which are restricted to their race.[1] Furthermore, most of the

Negroes who are members of denominations in which the white race predominates are separated into special conferences or districts while almost all of them are segregated into racial local churches. Only in a negligible number of instances are Negroes members of churches with a mixed racial constituency.[2]

This segregation of the races into racial denominations has not always prevailed. Prior to the Civil War—in the South at least but largely in the North also—white and black Christians worshipped together. They did not enjoy complete fellowship, it is true, but they participated in the same services and were members of the same denominations. Defenders of the old order are often able to draw a rather idyllic picture of the days before emancipation when "the two races mingled freely together, not on terms of social equality but in a very extended and constant social intercourse."[3] Domestic servants, if not plantation slaves, often shared with their masters and mistresses the ministrations of the same pastors and communed at the same Lord's Table. The Anglican Church was the leading denomination among the Southern masters and this church was officially very mindful of its duty toward the slaves, however inadequately its members may have practiced the ideals set forth by its bishops. As early as 1727 the bishop of London addressed a letter to masters and mistresses in the colonies, urging upon them the Christian duty of providing for the religious instruction of their slaves.[4] Many of his colleagues and successors repeated and reinforced his counsels.[5] The Society for the Propagation of the Gospel in Foreign Parts, which was established in London in 1701, had the evangelization of Negroes and Indians as a special objective. It worked in the colonies through the agencies of the established church for the religious instruction of the slaves; it sent missionaries to them and supported Negro schools; it even purchased two Negro youths whom it educated that they in turn might become teachers of Negro children. "Thus," as the Proceedings stated, "the Society hath opened a door by which the light of the blessed gospel will speedily and abundantly pour in among the poor negroes of Carolina." [6]

While the results of this missionary enterprise were not very great it is a noteworthy fact that Negroes who were baptized by the Episcopalian missionaries were brought into full membership with the church. The best known of these early missionaries, Rev. Samuel Thomas, reported in 1705 that on his quarterly visits to Goose Creek Parish in South Carolina he "always administered the Blessed Sacrament of the Lord's Supper, the number of communicants were about thirty, of which one was a Christian negro man." He observed also that twenty slaves came constantly to church.[7] The same report indicated that a similar situation existed in neighboring parishes. It is said that under the ministration of missionaries and friends Negroes began to attend church in such large numbers that they could not be accommodated and that in some congregations half of the attendants were Negroes. A report from Edenton,

North Carolina, a few years later contained the statement that "the blacks generally were induced to attend services at all these stations, where they behaved with great decorum." [8]   In the northern colonies similar conditions prevailed.   The Rev. Mr. G. Ross reported from Philadelphia that as many as twelve adult Negroes had been baptized after examination before the congregation.   At Newport more than one hundred Negroes "constantly attended the Publick Worship." [9]

Bishop Stephen Elliott of Georgia voiced the best ideals of the Episcopal church when in a convention address in 1847 he not only urged upon his church the necessity of increased attention to Negro missions but also expressed the earnest hope that "our Episcopal planters will take this matter into consideration and make arrangements for the employment of missionaries of their own church, so that masters and servants may worship together in unity of spirit and in the bond of peace.   It would tend very much to strengthen the relations of masters and slaves," he went on to say, "bringing into action the highest and holiest feelings of our common natures.   There should be much less danger of inhumanity on the one side, or of insubordination on the other, between parties who knelt upon the Lord's Day around the same table, and were partakers of the same communion." [10]

In some of the other denominations similar relations obtained between white and black Christians. The Presbyterian church, though less active than the

Episcopalian in missionary work among the slaves, yet demonstrated a great interest in the subject and like the English church sought to foster patriarchal relations between masters and servants in religion and on the plantation.[11] The General Assembly of 1854 commented on the increased zeal of its presbyteries in promoting the religious welfare of the slave population and noted that "in their houses of worship, provision at once special and liberal is made for the accommodation of the colored people, so that they may enjoy the privileges of the sanctuary in common with the whites."[12] The Southern branch of the church continued this patriarchal interest after separation from the North, affirming that "it is the peculiar mission of the Southern Church to conserve the institution of slavery, and to make it a blessing both to master and slave." The resolution continued, "We could not, if we would, yield up these four millions of immortal beings to the dictates of fanaticism and the menace of military power. We distinctly recognize the inscrutable Power which brought this benighted people into our midst, and we shall feel that we have not discharged our solemn trust until we have used every effort to bring them under the saving influence of the gospel of Christ."[13] When emancipation came the Southern church reaffirmed its historic policy by resolving "That whereas experience has invariably proved the advantages of the colored people and the white being united together in the worship of God, we see no reason why it should be otherwise now that they are freedmen and not slaves." It made provision for the organization of separate negro churches, "should our colored friends think it best to separate from us," [14] but resolved again in 1867, "that in the judgment of the Assembly, it is highly inexpedient that there should be any ecclesiastical separation of the white and colored races; that such a measure would threaten evil to both races, and especially to the colored." [15] So this church sought, vainly to be sure, to retain within its fold the ten thousand Negro communicants it reported at the close of the Civil War.[16]

Interest in the Negro on the part of the Presbyterian as well as of the Episcopal church had been stimulated by the great revival and by the democratic doctrines of the Revolution. Both of these had fostered the sense of equality and pricked the conscience of the churches on the subject of slavery.[17] It is intelligible, therefore, that the churches which were most strongly influenced by the revival and in closest touch with the radical wing of the democratic movement should have been readiest to welcome colored people as communicants. In the churches of the frontier the economic condition of pioneers, the heritage of the social gospel received from European churches of the poor and the absence of cultural or intellectual standards of church membership combined with the religious message and missionary zeal to make the ideal of racial brotherhood somewhat more effective than it could be among the conservative ecclesiastical groups. Thus the Cumberland Presbyterian church had about twenty thousand col-

ored members at the beginning of the Civil War.
"They belonged to the same congregations of which
white people were members, and sat under the ministry of the same pastors, though they had preachers
of their own race and often held separate meetings." [18] The history of the relation of the Methodist
church to the Negro is involved in the story of all the
social changes through which that church passed in
its progress from a sect of the disinherited to a
middle-class denomination with many slaveholders
among its members. As early as 1780, at the Baltimore Conference, provision was made for the meeting
of Negro classes under white leadership. The testimony borne by the church against slavery and its
efforts to exclude slaveholders from membership attracted the oppressed class and Methodism began to
gain Negro members. In 1799 one-fifth of its total
membership was Negro [19] and when the separation
of the Northern and Southern branches occurred in
1844 the Southern group alone accepted responsibility for 124,000 Negro communicants. By 1860 the
number of Negro Methodists in this branch had increased to 207,776, representing more than a fourth
of the total membership.[20] While the tendency toward a division of the races into distinct local
churches and conferences manifested itself among
Methodists and Baptists at a much earlier date than
among Presbyterians and Episcopalians, yet Wes-
leyanism fostered relatively close fellowship between
the two groups. This was the more easily accomplished in the early days of the American history

of the sect because of the relatively high social status of the free Negro in the last quarter of the eighteenth century and because most white Methodists at the time were recruited from the ranks of the economically poor and politically democratic classes. Among these the doctrines of equality and natural rights flourished and they were far less aware of class distinctions between the races than were the aristocratic Episcopalians and the middle-class Presbyterians.[21]

But it was in the Baptist churches especially that the Negroes shared with the white men the fellowship of the gospel. The reasons for the close relationship in this church were the same as those which prevailed in the Methodist denomination with the added attraction of free congregational polity. The latter feature permitted the Negroes to organize and govern their own churches and so provided them with a practical equality in religious affairs. The episcopalian structure of the Methodist church did not offer equal opportunities. Baptists were readier to extend the privileges of ordination to colored preachers than were other denominations. In the early annals of the Negro church the names of distinguished black Baptist preachers outnumber those of any other denomination. Occasionally the ministrations of these Negro preachers were accepted by white as well as by black Christians. So Josiah Bishop served for a brief time as pastor of a mixed Baptist church in Portsmouth, Virginia, and William Lemon was pastor of a white congregation at Gloucester in the same state.[22] "By 1810 . . . a number of large churches had been built up" in the Baptist denomination "by the labors of colored preachers; and most of the white churches had large numbers of colored members." [23]   Although separate colored churches were organized at an early date, yet prior to emancipation "the great mass of the colored Baptist membership was gathered in the white churches." [24]   Benedict's detailed *History of the Baptist Denomination*, published in 1846, contains many references to such churches. In 1831, for instance, the First Baptist Church of Richmond, Va., experienced a revival; "in a period of less than twelve months, more than 500 members were added, 217 of whom were white persons." The Third Church in the same city had 114 members, of whom 46 were colored persons. Of the Sunbury Association in Georgia this writer says that half of its twenty churches were wholly composed of colored people "and, with but few exceptions, they are much the most numerous in the other half." The Baptist Church in Natchez had 442 members of whom only 62 were white.[25]

Such was the prevailing condition of affairs before the Civil War. White and black worshipped together and, at their best, sought to realize the brotherhood Jesus had practiced and Paul had preached. There were many significant exceptions, it is true. But the general rule was that the two races should be united in religion. In the Protestant Episcopal and Presbyterian churches the relationship of masters and servants was of a patriarchal character. Many a master was sincerely interested in the temporal and eternal welfare of his charges and took paternal pride in their religious progress. It was not the virtue of democracy, the practice of equality, but the virtue of aristocracy, *noblesse oblige*, which was exercised in this relationship.[26] In the Methodist and Baptist churches, on the other hand, it was the conviction of the essential equality of all souls before God which inspired the white missionary and an occasional master to share the benefits of the common gospel in a common church with members of the other race.

Yet the religious unity of the two races was established and continued for a century for other reasons besides these ideal motives. The white man's fear of Negro independence was as important a factor in the matter as the white man's concern for the Negro's soul. In many instances the Negro was tolerated in the masters' church merely because such toleration was the less of two evils. The desirable good was the prevention of all contact with the spiritual and cultural influences of Christianity. The greater evil was the segregation of slaves into independent and uncontrolled organizations. From the beginning of the missionary enterprise among Africans many a master had been inimical to every effort at the conversion of his servants. The letter addressed in 1727 by the bishop of London to masters and mistresses answered various objections these had raised against religious propaganda among slaves. It had been argued that "the Time to be allowed for Instructing them would be an Abatement from the Profit of their Labor," "that making them Christians only makes them less diligent and more ungovernable," and that baptizing slaves automatically destroys the owner's property rights in them.[27] In the early period special weight was attached to the last objection, for it had been an unwritten law of Christendom that Christians might not hold fellow-believers as slaves. The slavery of the Negro had been defended, therefore, on the ground that he was a heathen. The slaveholder had felt the inconsistency of admitting an equality in religious relations which he was not willing to admit in civil life, and he had resented the efforts of missionaries to convert his servants as an attack on his property rights.[28] Most of the churches, in order that they might gain access to the Negroes with their missionary message, readily gave up the unwritten law and conciliated their own and the slaveholders' consciences by arguing with the good bishop "that Christianity, and the embracing of the Gospel, does not make the least Alteration in Civil property, or in any of the Duties which belong to Civil Relations; but in all these Respects, it continues Persons just in the same State as it found them. The Freedom which Christianity gives, is a Freedom from the Bondage of Sin and Satan, and from the Dominion of Mens Lusts and Passions and inordinate Desires; but as to their outward Condition, whatever that was before, whether bond or free, their being baptized and becoming Christians, makes no manner of Change in it." [29] Similar pronouncements on the part of other churchmen helped to overcome this objection of the slaveholders by convincing them that the old scruples against holding Christians as slaves were false, but it did not overcome their opposition to the evangelization of the Negro.[30]

Another objection loomed large in their minds. It was felt that the education which the slave might receive through the church and that the privileges which would be accorded to him as a Christian would only serve to reinforce his self-assertive tendencies, make him less docile a burden-bearer and incline him to a revolutionary spirit. This fear was greatly strengthened by the Haitian revolution and by various slave insurrections in the south, culminating in the Nat Turner uprising of 1831. It was true that many of the leaders of these insurrections were men who had received an inkling of the revolutionary doctrines of the New Testament and had learned what the claims and hopes of their humanity might be. Nat Turner had studied the Bible and religious literature especially and had started his insurrection in response to what he believed a divine communication. Negro churches were the meeting places of some revolutionary groups and examples were not wanting of converted and educated Negroes who displayed the undesired, self-assertive spirit.[31] The reaction of slave-holders and of the white race in general to such self-assertion expressed itself in attempts to deny to slaves all opportunity for contact with persons or ideas which might encourage in them the sense of human worth and the desire for freedom. Methodist and Baptist churches were especially suspect because of their early pronouncements against slavery. So the missionaries of these, but also of the other churches, were hard put to it to demonstrate to masters that the Christianization of slaves did not make them less but more slavish. "The Gospel," said the bishop of London, "everywhere enjoins, not only Diligence and Fidelity, but also Obedience for Conscience Sake . . . Christianity takes not out of the Hands of Superiors any Degrees of Strictness and Severity, that fairly appear to be necessary for the preserving Subjection and Government." [32]   A Methodist missionary from the West Indies pleaded that when the agitation for emancipation in England affected the slaves "as they learned chiefly through the violent speeches of their own masters or overseers what was going on in their favor . . . it was missionary influence that moderated their passions, kept them in the steady course of duty, and prevented them from sinning against God by offending against the laws of man. Whatever outbreaks or insurrections at any time occurred, no Methodist slave was ever proved guilty of incendiarism or rebellion for more than seventy years, namely from 1760 to 1833." [33]   Rev. C. C. Jones, leading Presbyterian advocate of negro missions, sought to win the goodwill of slaveholders by maintaining that slaves well instructed in the Christian faith were less likely to develop revolutionary inclinations than the half-educated, such as Nat Turner.[34]

Under the persuasion of such arguments and of their own conscience masters might yield a point and allow the slave to receive so much Christian instruction as would suffice for his salvation from Satan but not so much as might lead him to desire redemption from servitude. It was thought necessary, therefore, not only to prohibit the instruction of slaves in reading and writing but also to supervise their religious exercises carefully. This could best be done by requiring their attendance at the church of the master. Under the ministrations of a safe gospel preacher the slave might there receive a double insurance—against the doom of eternal bondage and against the damnation of temporal license. In many instances masters doubtless felt a genuine horror of the highly emotional, sometimes fantastic, religious practices of negroes left to themselves. They wished, for the good of the slave's soul, to have him inducted into the proprieties of a restrained faith and guarded against all infatuations. But that self-interest was largely responsible for the establishment of mixed churches is evident from the laws in the various Black Codes, especially from those passed after the Nat Turner insurrection. These often prohibited the assembling of more than five negroes, even for purposes of worship, without the permission of their masters, unless the services were in charge of some recognized white minister or observed by "certain discreet and reputable persons." [35]

Hence the association of white and black Christians in the various churches prior to the Civil War is scarcely to be regarded as a demonstration of the Christian principle of brotherhood and equality. On the contrary, the church relationship was in most instances designed to enlist the forces of religion in the task of preserving the civil relationship between masters and slaves. The former might indeed indulge their sense of virtue as they glanced at the galleries where their charges sat in due place and as they recalled the altruism of their interest in the souls of their servants. But the simultaneous reflection that the preacher's judicious use of St. Paul's epistles would inculcate into the bondsmen the virtues of obedience and diligence was not unwelcome to the minds of the owners of the troublesome hewers of wood and drawers of water.

The segregation of the races into distinct churches, was not, therefore, wholly a retrogressive step, involving the decline of a previous fellowship. Sometimes it was a forward step from an association without equality, through independence, toward the ultimately desirable fellowship of equals.

II

Every degree of fellowship was represented in the mixed churches and every degree of separation is represented in the schisms of the racial groups. The series of steps from fellowship to schism includes complete fellowship of white and Negro Christians in the local church, segregation within the local church, segregation into distinctly racial local churches with denominational fellowship, segregation into racially distinct dioceses or conferences with fellowship in the highest judicatories of the denomination, and, finally, separation of the races into distinct denominations. A still more detailed analysis of the stages of fellowship and schism between the races could be made by inquiring if fellowship, whether in local church, diocese or general assembly, includes equal privileges of participation in the government of the particular unit.

Complete fellowship without any racial discriminations has been very rare in the history of American Christianity. It has existed only where the number of Negroes belonging to the church was exceptionally small in proportion to the total membership, where the cultural status of the racial groups in the church was essentially similar, or where, as among some Quakers, racial consciousness was consciously overcome. In the mixed churches of the eighteenth and early nineteenth century some segregation of the races was the rule. Negroes, whether slaves or freedmen, were generally required to betake themselves, by means of a side door, to the gallery of the church or to some other section especially reserved for them. The slave gallery was as much of an institution in the house of God as in the theater. It had its uses, to be sure, and its defenders among Negroes as well as among the whites.[36] Yet it was a badge of white superiority and of colored inferiority before the throne of God; against it awakened Negroes could not but rebel. Frequently there was a separation of the congregations, the white minister holding a special service for negroes on Sunday afternoon or during the week. Such discriminations led, almost inevitably, to divisions of the local churches and to the establishment, as soon as the way was open, of separate white and colored organizations. Sometimes the whites took the initiative and excluded the negroes from their churches; more frequently the latter sought to demonstrate their religious independence by withdrawal from the Christian organizations which denied them equality. The latter step was generally possible before emancipation only in the North or among free Negroes; this was especially true after 1820 when the new importance of the slave and the fear of insurrection combined to impress upon the masters in the Southland the desirability of keeping their servants under close observation. But the movement toward separation has gone forward from the Revolution to the present day and the racial schism is still in process of completion.

Significantly enough these separations began shortly after the Revolution, when the doctrine of the rights of man raised high hopes among the Negroes, especially among the freedmen, and fostered an attitude of self-assertion among them. In Philadelphia Richard Allen, one of the greatest leaders of the Negro church, seceded with many colored followers from St. George Methodist Episcopal Church in 1787. Out of the Free African Society which he founded two independent Negro churches took their rise—Bethel Church (Methodist) and the African Protestant Episcopal Church of St. Thomas. In 1796 the John Street Methodist Episcopal Church of New York suffered a secession of Negroes who thereupon organized the African Methodist Episcopal Zion Church, mother church of the denomination which bears the same name. During the same period other independent Negro Methodist churches were organized on Negro initiative in Baltimore, Wilmington, Attleboro, Pa., Salem, N. C., Charleston, S. C., and in Vermont and New Hampshire. Independent Negro Baptist churches were established between 1776 and 1810 in Petersburg, Va., Richmond, Va., Savannah, Ga., Augusta, Ga., Lexington, Ky., and in New York, Philadelphia and Boston. Negro Episcopal congregations achieved separate organization at Philadelphia in 1794, at New York in 1818 and at Providence, New Haven and Detroit in the forties.[37]

In most of the instances mentioned the founding of the independent racial churches was due to the secession of negro members from mixed congregations. Examples are not lacking, however, of cases in which the white members of a church took the initiative in effecting segregation. When the First Baptist Church of Washington, D. C., was founded in 1802 it included many Negroes in its membership. But when a new church building was erected some years later the white members encouraged their colored brothers to continue to worship in the old meeting house. A similar separation took place in the First Baptist Church in Richmond when the white one-fourth of the membership moved to a new edifice, relinquishing the old building to the three-fourths of Negro membership. The African Baptist Church in Mobile, Ala., originated when the white members dissolved the old church and reorganized without the

Negroes. Similar situations were probably repeated by the score in the various denominations.[38]

The independent Negro churches which resulted from these secessions and exclusions were at first inclined to be loyal to the old denominations. But in time the same difficulties which had led to schisms of the local churches tended to divide the mixed denominations into racially distinct organizations. So the African Methodist Episcopal Church was organized under the leadership of Richard Allen as a distinct denomination in 1816 and the African Methodist Episcopal Zion Church became an independent sect in 1821.[39]

Powerful impetus toward the independent Negro church movement was given by the Civil War and emancipation. These stimulated a new sense of freedom, removed the restrictions which had prevented the organization of Negro churches in many states and released the energies of the former bondsmen. At the same time the after-effects of the struggle became apparent in the heightened caste-sense of the white people. Furthermore, Negro preachers showed themselves to be both more zealous and more effective evangelists of their own people than the white missionaries had been and Negro churches were organized rapidly under their leadership. From the Civil War onward the growth of the independent Negro church movement was accelerated by these various factors. The colored members of the Methodist Episcopal Church, South, deserted in large numbers to the A.M.E. and A.M.E. Zion Churches, which were now able to carry on their propaganda in the old slave states. Of the 208,000 colored members in the Southern Methodist Church in 1860 only 49,000 remained in 1866 when the General Conference gave the Negro membership permission to organize as a separate ecclesiastical body. This racial schism, which was probably desired by both parties, was consummated in 1870 and the Colored Methodist Episcopal Church was added to the list of denominations as the third great Negro church.[40] A fourth Negro denomination resulted from the division of the races in the Cumberland Presbyterian Church in 1869; another colored denomination took its rise in the separation of colored from white Baptists—a separation which began with the organization of Negro state conventions in the South immediately after the Civil War and which culminated in the organization of the National Baptist Convention in 1880. Even the Primitive and the Free Will Baptists divided. Yielding to the pressure exerted upon it, but not before it had lost a considerable proportion of its colored membership, the Northern Methodist Episcopal Church, while steadily refusing separation, in 1876 allowed its Negro pastors to organize distinctly racial conferences.[41] The Protestant Episcopal Church, like the Methodist, has resisted division but the long struggle of Negro missionary districts for independence from the white dioceses has continued to the present day and has resulted in the appointment of colored suffragan bishops for the government of Negro churches.

The result of these various schisms and separations appears in the continued growth of the Negro denominations from the Civil War to the present day, in the segregation of eighty-eight per cent. of Negro Christians into Negro denominations and of the great majority of the remainder into Negro conferences, separate for most practical purposes from their white denominational kinsmen. The racial schism instead of showing any signs of healing, as in the case of the sectional schisms and of the churches of the immigrants, is steadily growing more acute. Church union movements scarcely affect it. Projects for the union of the white churches or for the union of the colored churches only tend to accentuate the lines of division between the two groups.

III

The causes of the racial schism are not difficult to determine. Neither theology nor polity furnished the occasion for it. The sole source of this denominationalism is social; it demonstrates clearly the invasion of the church of Christ by the principle of caste. And this caste sense is, as always, primarily present in the economically and culturally superior group, and secondarily, by reaction, in the economically and culturally inferior society.

Negroes have apparently taken the initiative in forming separate churches, but the responsibility lies with their former masters in the North and South. These made the independent church movement inevitable by the attitude which they adopted toward the colored Christians. Their unquestioned assumption of superior privileges, their unconscious wounding of Negro self-respect, their complacent acceptance of the morality of the world as fitting for the church, have once more divided the body of Christ along the lines of social class. The white man's sense of superiority has come to expression in the assignment of Negroes to special places in the houses of worship, in refusals to admit him to equal privilege at the communion table, in the denial of ordination or of the right to participate in the government of the church and in the multitudinous affronts which special privilege unwittingly commits. In the situation it was but natural that the Negro should interpret every action, even though it was directed against an individual quite irrespective of his color, as an example of race discrimination. Caste hostility leads to inevitable suspicions and misunderstandings even in the church.

Thus the immediate occasion for the founding of the first Negro Methodist and Episcopalian churches was an affront offered to Richard Allen and his companions in St. George Methodist Episcopal Church in Philadelphia, when they were violently dealt with as they knelt at prayer in some part of the church they mistakenly supposed themselves privileged to occupy. "So," he wrote, "we all went out of the church in a body and they were no more plagued by us in the church." [42] The African Methodist Episcopal Zion Church of New York found one occasion for separation from the mixed racial church in the fact that "caste prejudice forbade their taking the sacrament until the white members were all served. This and the desire for other church privileges denied them caused them to organize among themselves." [43] Similar situations in other mixed churches led to separation as soon as the Negroes achieved sufficient liberty to make that step possible. The failure of denominations to admit colored preachers to full ordination, or to participation in church government or to eligibility to high office was further responsible for the Negro revolts.

Secession of Negroes from mixed churches was largely a movement of self-assertion on the part of the oppressed. Independence seemed a necessary prelude to equality. At all events segregation enabled them to escape the danger of having their legitimate self-respect constantly wounded by the superior pride of their fellow Christians. But there was a further reason for the schism of the races. It was the conviction of Negro leaders and of many white churchmen also that the religious welfare of the colored race required its independent ecclesiastical development. The mixed church under white hegemony was not designed either to prosecute missionary work effectively among Negroes nor to give these Christians that experience in self-government and leadership which their welfare required. Had it been possible to admit them to full participation in the work and worship of the church this argument would not have been cogent. Under the prevailing conditions of racial discrimination, however, separation seemed to be a wiser policy than the continued dependence of the Negro on white leadership. As in the case of Abram's and Lot's herdsmen agreement would have been best, but with peaceful co-operation impossible separation was better than continued strife or oppression.

Finally, the schism of the racial churches was and remains due to the difference in the culture levels of the two races. The Negroes, like the disinherited, required an emotional, empirical religion. "The heart depressed by drudgery, hardship, forlornness craves not merely moral guidance but exhilaration and ecstasy." Emotionalism in religion, however, was not only a reaction against the monotony and misery of laborious days on the plantation or in the factory; it was also the natural result of America's failure to provide the Negro with those educational opportunities which have brought about great changes in the religion of the disinherited and of the frontier.⁴⁴ With the increasing, though still sadly deficient, education of Negro children and with the rise of a cultured Negro class the colored churches have begun the transition from emotional naïveté to the doctrinal and ritual practices of the more sophisticated. Lay preachers are slowly giving way to a regular clergy, theological training of candidates for the ministry, though not yet the rule, is being emphasized more and more, while revivals and protracted meetings are being slowly eliminated in favor of educational methods of evangelization.

Such transitions to a common cultural level are

usually the prelude to the union of churches originally divided by class differences. But the cultural rise of the Negro holds out little hope for the unification of his churches with those of his whilom masters. Something more than a sociological cure seems necessary for the healing of this wound in the body of Christ. The color line has been drawn so incisively by the church itself that its proclamation of the gospel of the brotherhood of Jew and Greek, of bond and free, of white and black has sometimes the sad sound of irony, and sometimes falls upon the ear as unconscious hypocrisy—but sometimes there is in it the bitter cry of repentance.

CHAPTER TEN

WAYS TO UNITY

I

The history of schism has been a history of Christianity's defeat. The church which began its career with the promise of peace and brotherhood for a distracted world has accepted the divisions of the society it had hoped to transform and has championed the conflicts it had thought to transcend. It began its mission with the heroic proclamation of a new humanity "where there cannot be Greek and Jew, circumcision and uncircumcision, barbarian, Scythian, bondman, freeman," but where "Christ is all and in all." It has lost the radiant hopes and high desires of its vision-attended youth and, having accepted the cynical distinctions of the old humanity, it has maintained and reinforced these by its denominational structure, often giving the sanction of the spirit to the warfare of the flesh. From its position of leadership in the task of integrating humanity it has fallen to the position of a follower in a social process guided by economic and political forces. In its denominational aspect, at least, it has become part and parcel of the world, one social institution alongside of many others, a phase of the total civilization more frequently conditioned by other cultural tendencies than conditioning them. The old vision of the time when the kingdom of this world should be transformed into a kingdom of our Lord and of his Christ has faded into the light of a common day in which the brute facts of an unchanging human nature, of the invincible fortifications of economic and political society, of racial pride, economic self-interest and *Realpolitik* appear in their grim reality. The denominationalism which has been built on these foundations is the church's confession of defeat and the symbol of its surrender.

At the same time the victorious forces of divisiveness stand self-condemned in the moment of their triumph. Modern civilization, aghast at the results of a conflict between societies which had acknowledged no higher ideal than the pride of an ignorant nationalism, looks forward fearfully and almost helplessly to a yet mightier conflagration of the hates and passions it has nurtured. Remembering the holocaust which ethical stupidity ignited and science fed with fuel, it fears to face its foreboding of a yet more fateful application of the destructive knowledge which its warriors are feverishly seeking. It envisions the prospect of its death at its own hands. It contemplates the not impossible decline of its intellectual, religious, artistic, and economic activity into the unconscious, vegetative functioning of a race of fellaheen. It recalls and foresees the murder of its millions of young men, the destruction of its treasures, the enslavement of debt-ridden populations. And it knows that the way of divisive egotism is the way of doom. It regards the injustices of a class-organized, economic social order, which apportions its rewards neither according to merit nor to need, but according to the power of the strong to take the spoils; it looks upon the maddening rush of an acquisitive society intent upon the gain of possessions and yet more possessions, irrespective of their cost in spiritual and moral values; it begins to tremble before the mastery of the machine it has invented. It sees the growing fears, suspicions and hatreds of races long exploited by the nations of the West. And in its saner moments it becomes aware that it can save neither its self-esteem nor its existence nor yet the finer values its thinkers, prophets, artists and its toiling masses have wrought out, unless it is made captive to some compelling and integrating ideal which will restore to it a sense of the whole and will equip it with an ethics commensurate with the scope of its interests and of its world-embracing organization. The problem of the world is the problem of a synthesis of culture—of the building up of an organic whole in which the various interests and the separate nations and classes will be integrated into a harmonious, interacting society, serving one common end in diverse manners. Such a synthesis of culture can be built only upon a common world-view and a common ethics. Without these no civilization has flourished or left a contribution for the future. And every civilization which has possessed itself by possessing such a synthesis has received it from its religion.

For the simple and small world of Greece the religious ideal of the city-state sufficed. In it governor, warrior, artist, and artisan found their common *summum bonum*, transfigured by faith into a divine Athene and established upon the will of the gods. The medieval world was fashioned out of the remnants of empire and the raw materials of barbarism by the Catholic philosophy and ethics of the divine government. In these, the knowledge and the interests and the social life of the period were integrated, practically as well as theoretically, into a graded system, an organic whole. Compared with these ethical syntheses of its cultural forebears the modern world is atomic, confused, divided. It is at conflict with itself, for it knows of no supreme value to which it can subordinate the selfish desires of its groups and individuals and by means of which it can integrate its interests. The values to which it gives the greatest veneration and which it pursues with greatest abandon are values which inherently lead to strife and conflict. They are political and economic goods which cannot be shared without diminution and which arouse cupidity and strife rather than lead to co-operation and peace. Civilization, which has always in the past depended upon its religious faith for the discovery and assertion of its values, cannot produce out of itself the devotion to a common spiritual end which will unite rather than divide it. It pins its hopes on education and science but discovers that, while these are effective in propagating ideals previously accepted and in devising means for the attainment of acknowledged values, they are ineffective as methods for the revelation of ends or for securing for the supreme value the devout loyalty of the people. The synthesis of culture, the discovery of the *summum bonum*, and the growth of devotion to this divine value, wait now as always upon a faith that can arise only out of man's commerce with the ultimate realities of the cosmos. Civilization today must look to religion for the authoritative word which will enlist its forces in the co-operative, organic endeavor to achieve the highest good. But the dilemma of the Western world lies in the fact that while it depends upon religion for the creation of a common mind and the birth of a common loyalty, the only religion available seems incapable of establishing, even within its own structure, the desired harmony.

Hence there is abroad the cry for a new religion; homesick souls delude themselves with the belief that some Eastern temple, redolent with the incense of quiet centuries, will offer a refuge from the distractions of a divided world. But new religions do not rise at the call of need; if they do appear they come in organic, evolutionary continuity with the religions of the past which they absorb and reaffirm. And it is vain to look for salvation to an Eastern faith, whose thought-forms are strange, whose spirit is foreign, whose ideals and ideas are in radical opposition to the philosophy and the interests of the modern world. Amateurs of the foreign, sentimentalists and romanticists who have no regard for the facts of their own cultural heredity and are unaware of the massive power of customs, institutions, and the established tendencies of social history, may beguile themselves with the dream of grafting upon the progressive, activist, democratic, individualistic history of the West the quietistic, impersonal, metaphysical religion of the East with its ethics of a sad compassion. The realistic observer of social life, while acknowledging the æsthetic beauty of an Oriental creed, knows that the day is too far spent, the working day of the West too far advanced, for the realization of such a new dawn of Eastern light. He realizes that however great may be the distance between the creed and practice of Christendom, yet this civilization in its whole structure, from fundamental, unconscious ideas about personality and progress to the character of its economic and political life, has been conditioned by its religion. It can no more deny this fundamental factor in its cultural heredity than it can gainsay its biological sources. It is the product of its faith and by its faith it stands or falls.

II

Can that faith save the Western world? It is evident that it cannot do so in its present ecclesiastical forms, subject as these are to the very same influences which have brought civilization to its plight. Christianity as represented by denominations, which in turn are representative of the divided culture and its divisive interests, is no more able to stem the tide of disintegration in the world than it is able to set bounds to the process of disintegration within itself. Following the leadership of nationalism and capitalism, it cannot but continue the process of schism which has marked its entire past history.

It is true that under the influence of social forces which are arising out of the modern world, with the extension of communication, the passing of provincialisms, the rise of once suppressed economic groups to financial respectability and the acceptance on the part of a vast majority of such a population as the American of a standard common culture, old lines of cleavage are being erased and the possibilities of church union on the basis of a common social background are being established. The transition from cultural heterogeneity to cultural homogeneity on the part of the American people is reflected in the tendency of the various churches to accept a common attitude toward doctrine, a common piety, and a common type of worship. The social causes which divided the denominations of the immigrants and of the sections have long ceased to be operative in many churches which continue to maintain their separate existence merely because of the pure inertia of long-hallowed custom and denominational pride. But the existence of the social presuppositions of church union is no guarantee of its achievement. Some active motive sufficient to overcome denominational self-consciousness and inertia is required for the actual union of churches. Such a motive may be supplied in some instances by the necessity of competition, whether with larger Protestant groups or with Catholicism. Yet union achieved on this basis, as the outcome of the counsel of expediency, is of no significance as a moral factor in the ethical integration of civilization. The efficiency of churches as educational and self-propagating societies may be improved by mergers of this character; their ethical effectiveness is scarcely touched.

Sole reliance on social factors, moreover, cannot lead Christianity very far in achieving even an external union. The social process is as likely to bring about new schisms, or the accentuation of existing divisions, as it is to produce new alliances. The impact of nationalism and nationalist culture upon the churches may lead to the unification of denominations within the states but the same process may be responsible for the emphasis of differences between such national churches and for the dangerous division of organized Christianity along political lines. A movement toward nationalist churches is, in fact, evident everywhere in Christendom. Though state churches are passing, the integration of provincial, sectional, and class denominations into great popular organizations is in process in Europe and America, as also in the development of independent Indian, Chinese, and other Eastern churches.[1] Such churches, though separate from the state, are always in danger of representing the political and cultural interests of their nations more truly than a common, international Christianity. Desirable as is the organization of an American Protestant church from an ecclesiastical point of view, desirable also as is the growth of an indigenous Christianity in missionary lands, yet the development of these denominations may lead to an even greater subordination of Christian ethics to nationalist ethics than now prevails and to the opening up of more serious rifts in Christianity than now exist. The growth of such churches can be of ethical significance only if the social forces operative in their development can be brought under the control of the Christian ideal.

The continued division of the classes, which has been reflected in the rise of socialism as a religion—in Russia most of all but also in other European countries—will scarcely fail to issue in new schisms or in the increase of antagonism between this new faith of the poor and the religion of the upper classes, if social forces alone are allowed to determine the process of Christian history. It may be, indeed, that the continued prosperity of some nations, especially the United States, will tend to diminish the lines of division between the classes and so prevent the economic schism of religion. But it is no less probable that the coming of economic maturity and senescence with the exhaustion of raw materials, the increase of population and the growing power of a capitalist aristocracy will lead in the New World, as elsewhere, to the rise of antagonistic classes, which will assert their hostility in religious as well as in other forms. At all events the independent operation of economic and political forces no more guarantees the religious integrity of national life than it guarantees its economic and political unity. Far less does it provide for the international integration of Christianity and of humanity; in this sphere these factors alone are more likely to produce schism and new misunderstandings.

A wise leadership will avail itself of the social forces which make for union and will encourage the development of truly indigenous churches in missionary lands. It will not seek the impossible ideal of a church divorced from all of the cultural conditions of its environment. Least of all will it attempt to impress upon the Christianity of the Orient the purely European and American elements in the Western adaptations of the faith. But it will endeavor to find the line of distinction between the acceptance of merely cultural elements and the adoption or preservation of non-Christian social ethics— such as supreme devotion to the local state or to the interests and thought-forms of a social class. For helpful as the acceptance of a national language and of local forms of ritual or government may be in providing for the extension and inner assimilation of Christianity, just so perilous is the adoption of the ethics of a local nationalism, sectionalism, or racialism.

The determination of this line of division is ever one of the most difficult duties of the church. But it is not an impossible task. The individual Christian is confronted with the problem not only in the crises of nationalism, when he must determine the limits of his loyalty, but also in every adjustment which he is required to make to the economic and cultural society of which he is a part. Though he finds the decision difficult and always less than wholly Christian, he does not find it impossible. It would be far easier for him were he guided and supported in his decisions by a church which had made the attempt as a society to discover the principles which should determine the choices of individuals as well as of groups. And in many respects it is less difficult for the church to draw the line between a reasonable adjustment to social conditions and an un-Christian compromise than it is for the individual to do so. Group action in such matters is always more stable than individual action can be. Once the decision has been reached it is more likely to stand than it is in the case of the individual. In reaching its decision, also, the group finds larger support in tradition than does the individual, while the sense of group solidarity and power is no small aid in fostering the courage which is necessary for such a step. The difficulty of the task of finding the *via media* between adjustment to culture and compromise with prevailing social ethics cannot be an excuse for refusing to attempt it.

The problem itself points to the need of some other type of Christianity than the religion which merely adjusts itself to social conditions whether these make for union or for schism. The church which seeks universality by means of such adjustment sacrifices its claims to universality. It becomes an organization intent upon the promotion of its own interests, without a sense of its responsibility to the world as a social whole. And it loses its integrity in the very process of seeking universality, because its adjustments are made to a world which, far from being a universe, is divided in many ways. A universalism which is sought by adaptation only defeats itself.

Denominational Christianity, that is a Christianity which surrenders its leadership to the social forces of national and economic life, offers no hope to the divided world. Lacking an integrating ethics, lacking a universal appeal, it continues to follow the fortunes of the world, gaining petty victories in a war it has long lost. From it the world can expect none of the prophetic guidance it requires in its search for synthesis.

III

There is another type of Christianity which is quite as ineffective though perhaps not as destructive in its contacts with civilization as is denominational Christianity. The other-worldly faith which regards the message of the gospel as applying to the individual's relation to a transcendental sphere alone and condemns every aspect of the present world, including culture, religious striving, and every attempt at amelioration of social evils as the expression of a depraved and lost will, has been resurrected today by the crisis theology of Germany and is receiving no small attention throughout Christendom. It has become a refuge for disillusioned followers of the social gospel, who have noted how much of evil may

lurk in every attempted reformation, how stubborn
are the instincts of individual and collective humanity, how much of hypocrisy is associated with every
effort to realize the ethics of the gospel. Once more
the old doctrine of the Reformation is emphasized:
man and all his works are evil; there is none good
save God. The only hope of men lies in the miracle
of divine mercy and the only promise of the
kingdom of God that men can cherish is the
promise of a radical, cosmic revolution which will
substitute for the present world with its natural laws
as well as its social evils a new heaven and a new
earth entirely different from the cosmos as it now
exists. Every human effort, whether it be that of
religion or of ethics, is not only futile but damnable.

Valuable as the other-worldly, transcendental version of Christian theology is, necessary as it appears
as the complement of a frequently provincial social
gospel, important as every individual finds its conclu-
sions in his religious life, yet it appears simply
irrelevant so far as the social task of Christianity is
concerned. It is true that the eternal fate of every
individual is hopeless save that divine mercy purge
his compromises, forgive his sins, fulfil his thwarted
desires after goodness, and redeem him from the
destruction that lurks within. It is true that the
ultimate, cosmic significance of the kingdom of God
must far transcend all mundane versions of the ideal
for which men labor. Yet is there no relationship
between these ideals and the cosmic fact? Is there no
continuity between the divine mercy and those angels

of man's better nature which struggle with the
demons of the jungle in his individual and corporate
life? Whatever be the final outcome for the individual or for society—and this the religious man
cannot but leave in the hands of God—the duty of
dealing with the present world in the light of our
highest ideals and best insights remains inescapable.
And the situations in the "here and now" do not
yield to the simple device of condemning, as equally
sinful, the reformation and the evil to be reformed,
the search for unity and the division to be overcome.
Between the white and black of absolute good and
absolute evil there are infinite numbers of shades of
gray and between any two of these shades there may
be vast and important distinctions. The church cannot escape responsibility for the present order of civilization by referring men to some transcendental
sphere where all their efforts are revealed as equally
marked with guilt and imperfection. There remain
in addition to the realms of perfection and sin various
degrees of imperfection, of justice and injustice.
To say, as the crisis theology says, that religion as a
human enterprise stands self-condemned by its mundane and human character is to ignore the obligation
which lies upon religion, just as a human enterprise,
to substitute the better for the good or the less bad
for the bad and to penetrate the stuff of existence,
so far as possible, with so much of saving knowledge
and so much of redeeming effort as are available.
To anticipate attainment too easily has ever been a
weakness of religion; to anticipate the attainment

of peace with God by reliance on His mercy rather than on human effort is an inescapable necessity; but to anticipate the attainment of His righteous rule by reliance on eschatological miracle and meanwhile to condemn all efforts to work out human salvation by the best endeavor of which men are capable, is to reduce religion to an ethical anodyne.

If denominational Christianity is surrender to the world, this sort of theological Christianity is escape from the world. Neither variety offers any hope for the church or for mundane humanity. Is there not available some form of the Christian faith which possesses both the compelling ideal that can bring inner unity to the world and courage to undertake the penetration of human society with that ideal despite the difficulties and confusions which tempt to surrender or to flight?

IV

The Christianity of the gospels doubtless contains the required ideal. Its purpose is not the foundation of an ecclesiastical institution or the proclamation of a metaphysical creed, though it seeks the formation of a divine society and presupposes the metaphysics of a Christlike God. Its purpose is the revelation to men of their potential childhood to the Father and their possible brotherhood with each other. That revelation is made not in terms of dogma but of life, above all in the life of Christ. His sonship and his brotherhood, as delineated in the gospel, are not the example which men are asked to follow if they will, but rather the demonstration of that character of ultimate reality which they can ignore only at the cost of their souls. The *summum bonum* which this faith sets before men is nothing less than the eternal harmony of love, in which each individual can realize the full potentiality of an eternal life in self-sacrificing devotion to the Beloved Community of the Father and all the brethren.

The appeal of that ideal to the world is unmistakable. Adumbrated by social and ethical science, gropingly anticipated even by economics, illustrated in the life of the family at its best, allegorized in the nobler aspects of patriotism, fumblingly essayed in endless political experiments, seen in the dark glass of reason by philosophers and prophets, it is the unknown good which men have ignorantly worshipped and long sought after that haply they might find it. The Christian ideal wakes an answering response in many a human heart. It is able to command a loyalty far deeper and more extensive than that which the church in its mundane aspects can claim. Leaders of Oriental nationalism and Western socialism, remote though they may be from the church and its dogma, are often not far from this ideal of the kingdom of heaven. Among the masses of men betrayed into useless toil and murderous warfare by the ethics of the world, the yearning for a fairer social order is frequently readier to accept the guidance of this faith than the cynical counsel of self-interest and class warfare. Throughout mankind there is a vast fund of latent energy and devotion which awaits release and guidance by such an ideal as that of the Gospels. In this ideal of the highest good, in this world-view of the kingdom of love and in this conception of the ethical life of men, if anywhere, there is the available material for the creative synthesis of human culture and for the organic integration of mankind into a functional whole.

For the proclamation of this Christianity of Christ and the Gospels a church is needed which has transcended the divisions of the world and has adjusted itself not to the local interests and needs of classes, races, or nations but to the common interests of mankind and to the constitution of the unrealized kingdom of God. No denominational Christianity, no matter how broad its scope, suffices for the task. The church which can proclaim this gospel must be one in which no national allegiance will be suffered to infringe upon the unity of an international fellowship. In it the vow of love of enemy and neighbor and the practice of non-resistance will need to take their place beside the confession of faith and the rites. For without complete abstention from nationalist ethics the universal fellowship of this church would inevitably fall apart into nationalist groups at the threat of war or under the influence of jingoistic propaganda. In such a church distinctions between rich and poor will be abrogated by the kind of communism of love which prevailed in the early Jerusalem community. This communism differs as radically from the dictatorship of the prole-

tariat as it does from the dictatorship of capitalism. The principle of harmony and love upon
which it alone can be established requires that each
contribute to the community according to his ability
and receive from it according to his need, not according to some predetermined principles of quanti-
tative equality or of privilege. Furthermore, this
church of love will need to bridge the chasm between
the races, not only by practising complete fellowship
within the house of God but by extending that
practice into all the relationships of life. It will
need to mediate the differences of culture by supplying equality of opportunity to tutored and untutored alike and by giving each their share in the
common task and in the common love.

Only such a church can transcend the divisions of
men and by transcending heal them; only such a
church can substitute for the self-interest and the
machinery of denominationalism the dominant desire
for the kingdom and its righteousness and the free
activity of familiar fellowship. It requires from its
members the sacrifice of privilege and pride and bids
each count the other better than himself. It can
plant within the nations a fellowship of reconciliation which will resist the animosities nurtured by
strife for political and economic values—a fellowship which, doubtless, may often be required to carry
crosses of shame and pain when the passions of men
have been aroused for conflict.

To describe such a church, it will be objected, is
only to describe another sect, which will be added to

the denominations and increase the confusion. But
the church of fellowship in love need never be a sect.
Rather it has always existed as a church within the
churches. It is no mere vision born of desire. It is
a fellowship with a long history and a record of many
victories. It flourished in the primitive church of
Jerusalem, where all were one in Christ. It came to
appearance in the brotherhood of the early friars
under Francis' leadership. It has functioned in
every movement of mercy and reconciliation. The
sects which it has founded have failed to hold fast to
the ideal and have become partisan champions of a
provincialized gospel. They have succumbed to the
interests which corporate societies must take in their
own welfare and existence. They have sought to
transmit the heritage of the spirit through inelastic
rules and creeds which often have come to belie their
original meaning. But though its sects have failed,
the fellowship has continued. Again and again it has
been the creative center of movements of the spirit
which have penetrated the world. The band of
disciples, the communities of Jerusalem and Antioch, did not fail when the sect of Jewish Christianity
perished. The fellowship of love which had been
nurtured among them impressed its ideals upon the
ancient world. It did not change the whole world
into conformity with its own pattern, to be sure,
but it gave its savor, through the mediation of Paul,
to the institutions of society so that family life, the
relations of masters and slaves, and of the races were

at least partially redeemed. The little brothers of the poor brought their influence to bear upon the medieval world in like manner. The Franciscan order was a failure, but the Franciscan movement which spread out from Portiuncula to the whole Catholic world was one of the great victorious marches of history. It penetrated palace and hovel, reviving practical piety and inscribing the grace of charity on hearts brutalized by centuries of war and oppression. The influence of George Fox and his Friends is not commensurable with the success of the Society in gaining members. The savor of friendship has penetrated from that source into regions untouched by the sect. Slavery has had to give way before it; the relations of employers and employees have been affected by it; the conscience of men at war has again and again been pricked by its example. There have been countless other, less dramatic appearances of the fellowship of love, but for the most part it does its work quietly, in hospitals under the tropical sun or in the icy north, in prisons where lovers of peace atone for the hatreds of war, in industrial establishments where owners and workers have learned to share their problems and their profits, in all the incidental and countless human contacts of men divided by color, tradition or estate.

The increase of that fellowship today is the hope of Christendom and of the world. It is the church which can save the churches from the ruin of their secularism and consequent division. It challenges the world to recall its better nature and to find unity and peace in the knowledge of the divine love upon which all stable and just social life must be built.

The road to unity which love requires denominations, nations, classes, and races to take is no easy way. There is no short cut even to the union of the churches. The way to the organic, active peace of brotherhood leads through the hearts of peacemakers who will knit together, with patience and self-sacrifice, the shorn and tangled fibers of human aspirations, faiths, and hopes, who will transcend the fears and dangers of an adventure of trust. The road to unity is the road of repentance. It demands a resolute turning away from all those loyalties to the lesser values of the self, the denomination, and the nation, which deny the inclusiveness of divine love. It requires that Christians learn to look upon their separate establishments and exclusive creeds with contrition rather than with pride. The road to unity is the road of sacrifice which asks of churches as of individuals that they lose their lives in order that they may find the fulfilment of their better selves. But it is also the road to the eternal values of a Kingdom of God that is among us

NOTES

CHAPTER ONE

1 I Corinthians 12.

2 John 17.

3 Cf. Harnack, *Expansion of Christianity*, Vol. I, pp. 68-70, 181-249; Troeltsch, *Soziallehren der Christlichen Kirchen und Gruppen*, pp. 49-58.

4 Cf. Sombart, *Quintessence of Capitalism*, pp. 267-268.

5 Weber, *Gesammelte Aufsätze zur Religionssoziologie*, I, 153, 211; Troeltsch, *Soziallehren der Christlichen Kirchen und Gruppen*, pp. 362 ff.

6 *Ecclesiastical Records of the State of New York*, Vol. VI, pp. 4292 f.

CHAPTER TWO

1 For a discussion of the economic theories of the Reformation and for the literature on the subject see Preserved Smith, *Age of the Reformation*, Ch. XIV.

2 Troeltsch, *op. cit.*, p. 27.

3 Cf. Kautsky, *Geschichte des Sozialismus in Einzeldarstellungen;* the best collection of material on the social status of early Christians is to be found in Harnack, *The Expansion of Christianity in the First Three Centuries*, trans. by James Moffatt, London, 1904. For a discussion of the proletarian character of early Christianity as set forth by socialist historians, see Troeltsch, *op. cit.*, note pages 22-24. Troeltsch points out here that the mass of early Christians were not the impoverished proletarians of Rome but members of the free laboring groups found in the eastern part of the empire.

4 Cf. Harnack, *Expansion of Christianity in the First Three Centuries*, Vol. I, p. 106 *et passim.*

5 On the relationship of the Peasant Revolt and the Anabaptist movement see Belfort Bax, *Rise and Fall of the Anabaptists*, pp. 2, 26 f., 330; Troeltsch, *Soziallehren*, pp. 812 f. The earlier phase of the Peasant Revolt was under the influence of Anabaptist teachers, but its later, violent phase was inspired partly by Hussites and Taborites while the majority of Anabaptists took the position of non-resistance. Cf. also Bax, *The Peasants War in Germany.*

NOTES

6 Luther's *Werke, Kritische Gesammtausgabe*, Weimar, Vol. 18, 1908, p. 309.

7 *Ibid.*, pp. 361, 358; cf. also Vol. XVII, pp. 265 f.

8 Cf. Smith, *Age of the Reformation*, p. 558; H. T. Andrews, "The Social Principles and Effects of the Reformation," in *Christ and Civilization*.

9 Smith, *op. cit.*, p. 100.

10 *Ibid.*, p. 154.

11 Bax, *op. cit.*, pp. 63 f.

12 The best treatment of the social and religious revolution in seventeenth-century England is to be found in Gooch, *The History of English Democratic Ideas in the Seventeenth Century*, London, 1898. Other important discussions of the period are: R. Barclay, *The Inner Life of the Religious Societies of the Commonwealth*, London, 1878; Canon Henson, *English Religion in the Seventeenth Century*, London, 1903; Berens, L., *The Digger Movement in the Days of the Commonwealth, as revealed in the Writings of Gerald Winstanley, etc.*, London, 1906; Pease, T. C., *The Leveller Movement*, Washington, 1916; Burrage, *The Early English Dissenters*, Vol. I.

13 McGiffert, *Protestant Thought Before Kant*, p. 96.

14 Calvin, *Institutes*, Book IV, Ch. XX, Sec. 27.

15 Quoted in Gooch, *op. cit.*, p. 169.

16 Selbie, *English Sects. A History of Nonconformity*, p. 89.

17 Barclay, *op. cit.*, p. 181.

18 Gooch, *op. cit.*, p. 127.

19 *Ibid.*, p. 131.

20 Calamy, *Life of Baxter*, abridged, London, 1702, pp. 87, 90.

21 Howells' *Letters*, ed. Jacob, p. 337. Quoted in Gooch, p. 130.

22 Clarendon's *History*, Vol. X, p. 175.

23 Gooch, p. 141.

24 Milton's *Eikonoklastes*, Preface.

25 Cf. Gooch, p. 260.

26 Tawney, *Religion and the Rise of Capitalism*, p. 212. On the transition see especially Troeltsch, *Soziallehren*, pp. 779 ff.

27 Cf. Gooch, pp. 212 ff.

28 Gooch, pp. 123 ff., 206 ff.

29 *Ibid.*, p. 87.

30 Quoted in Pease, *Leveller Movement*, note p. 77.

31 From Preface to "Watchword to the City of London," quoted in Gooch, p. 221.

32 Pell's *Correspondence*, Vol. I, 155; Gooch, p. 263.

33 Quoted in Gooch, p. 265.

34 Pagitt, *Heresiography*, p. 244, quoted in Gooch, p. 272.

35 Gooch, p. 272.

36 Cf. Gooch, p. 263.

37 Cf. Troeltsch, "Die Englischen Moralisten," etc. *Gesammelte Schriften*, Vol. IV, pp. 394 ff.

38 *Watchword to the City of London;* quoted in Gooch, p. 221 f.

NOTES

39 Quoted in Berens, *The Digger Movement*, p. 45.

40 Cf. Pease, *The Leveller Movement;* Troeltsch, *Soziallehren,* note pp. 821-822; Gooch, p. 142.

41 Calamy, *An Abridgement of the Life of Baxter,* p. 102.

42 Quoted in Gooch, p. 220.

43 *The True Levellers Standard Advanced,* 1649. Quoted in Gooch, p. 217.

44 Quoted in Gooch, p. 265. On the Fifth Monarchy Men, see Gooch, pp. 260-267; Simpkinson, *Major-General Harrison;* Troeltsch, *Soziallehren,* p. 818.

45 Gooch, p. 278.

46 Cf. Troeltsch, *Soziallehren,* pp. 913 ff., 946 ff.

CHAPTER THREE

1 Barclay, *The Inner Life of the Religious Societies of the Commonwealth,* pp. 546 ff.

2 Cf. Weber, *Gesammelte Aufsätze zur Religionssoziologie,* Vol. I, pp. 163 ff.; on the Quakers, cf., pp. 150 ff.

3 Lecky, *A History of England in the Eighteenth Century,* London, 1899, Vol. III, pp. 51, 13 f. Lecky's account of the social background of Methodism, in the eighth chapter of his great history, is highly instructive from the point of view of the present work. See also Southey, *Life of Wesley,* Ch. IX.

4 Fisher, *History of Christian Doctrine,* N. Y., 1896, pp. 389 f.

5 Lecky, Vol. I, pp. 93 ff.

6 Quoted in Fisher, p. 390.

7 Lecky, Vol. III, pp. 18 f.

8 *Ibid.,* Vol. III, p. 147.

9 Wesley's *Works,* N. Y. 1833, Vol. V, pp. 250 f.

10 Letter by a Gentleman of Pembroke College. Quoted in Tyerman, *Life and Times of the Rev. John Wesley, A.M., Founder of the Methodists,* Vol. I, pp. 455 ff.

11 Hutton's *Memoirs,* p. 42. Quoted in Tyerman.

12 Cowper's "Truth."

13 Lecky, III, pp. 121 ff.

14 *Ibid.,* p. 100.

15 Quoted in Tyerman, Vol. I, p. 277.

16 Cf. T. C. Hall, "The Evangelical Revival and Philanthropy," in the composite work, *Christ and Civilization,* London, 1912, pp. 377-408. Lecky, Vol. III, pp. 147-148. W. H. Meredith, "John Wesley, Christian Socialist," *Methodist Review,* May-June 1901.

17 Quoted in Tyerman, Vol. I, p. 494.

18 Wesley's *Works,* V, p. 193.

19 Cf. Hall, "The Evangelical Revival and Philanthropy" in *Christ and Civilization.*

20 Quoted in Southey, Vol. II, p. 305 f. (Ch. XXIX.)

21 Cf. Troeltsch, *Soziallehren,* pp. 839 f.

NOTES

CHAPTER FOUR

[1] Weber, *Gesammelte Aufsätze zur Religionssoziologie*, Vol. I, pp. 239 f.

[2] Sombart, *Quintessence of Capitalism*, pp. 267-268.

[3] Weber, *op. cit.*, pp. 256 ff.; cf. Tawney, *Religion and the Rise of Capitalism*, pp. 230-231.

[4] Tawney, *op. cit.*, p. 112, cf. p. 108; Weber, *op. cit.*, pp. 89 ff. and 124 ff., offers a detailed analysis of the social effects of the doctrine; Wuensch, *Evangelische Wirtschaftslehre*, pp. 327 ff., emphasizes the importance of Calvin's conception of God as active and sovereign rather than of the specific doctrine of predestination.

[5] Cf. Tawney, *op. cit.*, pp. 227-253.

[6] Tawney, *op. cit.*, p. 230.

[7] On the relation of Catholicism to the ethics of the bourgeoisie cf. Wuensch, *Evangelische Wirtschaftsethik*, 300-315; Tawney, *Religion and the Rise of Capitalism*, Ch. I; Troeltsch, *Gesammelte Schriften*, Vol. I, Ch. 2, Pt. 8, esp. pp. 342-350; Weber, *op. cit.*, 17 ff.; Sombart, in *The Quintessence of Capitalism*, defends a point of view opposite to that of these authorities. He regards Catholicism as favorable, Protestantism as inimical to the new commerce; cf. especially pp. 251-252.

[8] Cf. Weber, Vol. I., pp. 26-28.

[9] The theory of Weber, which Tawney criticises but in part follows, that Calvinism is the parent of capitalism, is subject to considerable questioning. Wuensch in his *Evangelische Wirtschaftslehre* points out that Calvinism may indeed have affected industrialism strongly but that rationalism is more likely to have been responsible for the parentage of capitalism; cf. pp. 336-346. The theory adopted in this chapter is that we are dealing with interacting phases of a culture rather than with a relation of cause and effect, operating in one direction only.

[10] Tawney, p. 230; cf. Dowden, *Puritan and Anglican*, p. 23.

[11] Tawney, *op. cit.*, pp. 104 ff.; 131; Troeltsch, *Gesammelte Schriften*, Vol. I, p. 636; Vol. IV, pp. 146 f.; Sombart, *The Jews and Modern Capitalism*, pp. 248 f.

[12] Wuensch, *op. cit.*, p. 339; cf. Troeltsch, Vol. I, p. 718.

[13] See above, notes 7 and 9.

[14] Tawney, *op. cit.*, pp. 115-132; cf. pp. 211-227. McGiffert, *Protestant Thought Before Kant*, pp. 91 f.

[15] Tawney, *op. cit.*, p. 132.

[16] *Ibid.*, pp. 226 f.

[17] Cf. Troeltsch, *Gesammelte Schriften*, Vol. I, pp. 683 ff.; 733 ff.

[18] *Ibid.*, pp. 703, 755 ff.; Vol. IV, pp. 145 ff.

[19] Cf. Edmundson, *History of Holland*, p. 113; Oechsli, *History of Switzerland*, pp. 208 ff.

[20] Tawney, *op. cit.*, p. 227; cf. pp. 113, 226; cf. Troeltsch, Vol. I, pp. 704-722.

NOTES

21 Wuensch, *op. cit.*, pp. 343-345.

22 Dowden, *Puritan and Anglican*, p. 276.

23 *Ibid.*, p. 275.

24 Gilbert Seldes, *The Stammering Century*, offers many interesting sidelights and helpful interpretations of this process.

CHAPTER FIVE

1 For lists of American denominations see Winchester, *The Handbook of the Churches;* and U. S. Census Reports, Religious Bodies, 1926.

2 Ripley, *The Races of Europe*, cf. p. 33.

3 Cf. Harnack, *Geschichte der Christlichen Religion* in *Kultur Der Gegenwart*, Pt. I, Sec. IV, pp. 151-159.

4 Guignebert, *Christianity*, pp. 186-187.

5 Article, "Orthodox Eastern Church," Encyc. Brit., 11th ed., Vol. XX, p. 337.

6 Stanley, *History of the Eastern Church*, pp. 90 f.; cf. Loofs, *Symbolik*, pp. 77-106.

7 Adeney, *The Greek and Eastern Churches*, pp. 230 ff.

8 Cf. Workman, *Christian Thought to the Reformation*, Ch. IV; G. P. Fisher, "The Old Roman Spirit and Religion in Latin Christianity" in *Discussions in History and Theology*.

9 Bonwetsch, *Griechisch-Orthodoxes Christentum und Kirche*, in *Kultur der Gegenwart*, Pt. I, Sec. iV, p. 169. Loofs, *Symbolik*, pp. 113, 117.

10 Cf. Article, "Orthodox Eastern Churches," Enc. Britannica, 13th ed., Vol. II, pp. 1133 ff.; cf. also Loofs, *op. cit.*, pp. 112-118; Adeney, *op. cit.*, pp. 340-354.

11 Adeney, *op. cit.*, p. 353.

12 Mueller, *Christentum und Kirche Westeuropas im Mittelalter*, in *Kultur der Gegenwart*, Pt. I, Sec. IV, p. 199.

13 *Ibid.*, pp. 203-210.

14 Mueller, *op. cit.*, pp. 285-288. Smith, *Age of the Reformation*, pp. 41 ff.

15 Mueller, *op. cit.*, pp. 288-290.

16 Cf. Taylor, *The Medieval Mind*, passim.

17 Smith, *op. cit.*, pp. 5, 549.

18 Troeltsch, *Protestantisches Christentum und Kirche in der Neuzeit*, in *Kultur der Gegenwart*, Pt. I, Sec. IV, p. 624.

19 *Ibid.*, pp. 488-489, 529-532.

20 See above, pp. 17 ff.

21 Vedder, *Reformation in Germany*, Pt. III, Ch. II.

22 Lindsay, *History of the Reformation*, Vol. II, pp. 360, 363 f., 411, 413 f.

23 *Ibid.*, pp. 303 f.

24 Romans 13, 1.

25 On the ethics of nature and Christian ethics see Troeltsch, *Gesammelte Schriften*, Vol. I, pp. 156 ff., 532 ff., 661 ff.

NOTES

²⁶ Cf. Troeltsch, *Protestantisches Christentum und Kirche in der Neuzeit,* pp. 488 ff.

CHAPTER SIX

¹ Turner, *The Frontier in American History,* p. 38.

² *Ibid.,* p. 30.

³ Cf. Beard, *Rise of American Civilization,* Vol. I, p. 88.

⁴ Paxson, *History of the American Frontier, 1763-1893,* p. 102; Turner, *op. cit.,* pp. 205 f.

⁵ Beard, *op. cit.,* pp. 266 f., 349 ff., 507 ff., 542 ff.; cf. Paxson, Chs. XII, XXVIII.

⁶ Turner, *op. cit.,* pp. 109 f.

⁷ Turner, *op. cit.,* p. 345; Paxson, *op. cit.,* p. 115; Tracy, *The Great Awakening,* pp. 217-218; cf. Davenport, *Primitive Traits in Religious Revivals,* pp. 64 f.

⁸ Cleveland, Catharine, *The Great Revival in the West,* pp. 29 f.; McNeill, "Religious and Moral Conditions Among Canadian Pioneers," *Papers of the American Society of Church History, Second Series,* Vol. VIII, pp. 65 ff.

⁹ Cf. L. W. Bacon, *History of American Christianity,* pp. 222-223; cf. Newman, *History of the Baptist Churches in the United States,* pp. 304-305.

¹⁰ Tiffany, *A History of the Protestant Episcopal Church in the United States of America,* pp. 40 ff.

¹¹ *Ibid.,* p. 78.

¹² Cf. Van Tyne, *England and America,* Lecture III—"The Anglican Church and the Dissenters in the American Revolution." Van Tyne makes the statement that eighty per cent. of the patriots were Dissenters, and seventy-five per cent. of the Loyalists, Episcopalians.

¹³ Cf. Bacon, *op. cit.,* pp. 308 f.

¹⁴ Bacon, *op. cit.,* pp. 96, 99 f.; Walker, *History of the Congregational Churches in the United States,* pp. 100 ff.

¹⁵ Walker, *op. cit.,* p. 98.

¹⁶ Bacon, *History of American Christianity,* p. 104. On the class structure of colonial society, see Beard, *Rise of American Civilization,* Vol. I, pp. 125 ff.

¹⁷ Quoted in Turner, *The Frontier in American History,* p. 64.

¹⁸ Cf. Turner, *op. cit.,* pp. 42-43; Mode, *Frontier Spirit in American Christianity,* pp. 48 f.

¹⁹ On the Great Awakening, see Tracy, *The Great Awakening;* Jonathan Edwards, *Narrative of Surprising Conversions.*

²⁰ Quoted in Tracy, *op. cit.,* pp. 287 f.

²¹ *Ibid.,* pp. 304-305.

²² Walker, *op. cit.,* p. 262; cf. Tracy, *op. cit.,* pp. 315-325, 409 ff.

²³ Tracy, *op. cit.,* pp. 307 f.

²⁴ Bacon, *op. cit.,* pp. 173 f.; Newman, *A History of the Baptist Churches in the United States,* p. 245. Cf. Backus, *Church His-*

tory of New England from 1620 to 1804, Phila., 1839, pp. 176 ff. Backus, *History of New England*, Vol. II, cc. XIV-XVIII.

25 Walker, *op. cit.*, p. 318.

26 Quoted in Beard, *op. cit.*, Vol. I, p. 527.

27 Cf. Paxson, *The Great Awakening in the Middle Colonies*, pp. 24 ff.

28 "Protestation of 1741." *Records of the Presbyterian Church in the United States of America, 1706-1788*, pp. 157 ff.

29 Thompson, *Presbyterian Churches in the United States*, p. 88.

30 *Ibid.*, pp. 89 f.

31 Bacon, *History of American Christianity*, p. 186.

32 *Ibid.*, p. 332.

33 McDonnold, B. W., *History of the Cumberland Presbyterian Church*, 3rd ed., 1893, pp. 39-81; cf. Davidson, *History of the Presbyterian Church in Kentucky*, pp. 223-263; Cleveland, *The Great Revival in the West*, pp. 143-147.

34 Davidson, *op. cit.*, pp. 190 ff.; Cleveland, *op. cit.*, pp. 134 ff.

35 Davidson, *op. cit.*, pp. 203, 207 ff.; Cleveland, *op. cit.*, pp. 141 ff.

36 Cf. Seldes, *The Stammering Century.*

37 Thompson, *op. cit.*, pp. 69-71. Cf. Bacon, *op. cit.*, pp. 332-333.

38 Cf. Bacon, *op. cit.*, p. 292 ff.

39 Cf. Bacon, *op. cit.*, pp. 228-229. *Am. Ch. Hist. Series*, Vol. VIII, pp. 304 ff., Vol. XII, pp. 317 ff., 385 ff.

CHAPTER SEVEN

1 Thomas, *History of the Society of Friends, American Church History Series*, Vol. XII, pp. 236-241; cf. Bacon, *op. cit.*, pp. 138 f. 149; cf. Mode, *The Frontier Spirit in American Christianity*, pp. 93-95.

2 *Ecclesiastical Records of the State of New York*, Vol. I, pp. 399 f.

3 Bacon, *op. cit.*, pp. 173 f.; Newman, *A History of the Baptist Churches in the United States*, p. 245.

4 Newman, *op. cit.*, p. 271; cf. Backus, *Church History of New England*, pp. 225 ff.

5 Newman, *op. cit.*, pp. 282-283.

6 *Ibid.*, Chs. III and IV.

7 Newman, *op. cit.*, pp. 291, 296 ff., 301, 334, *et passim.*

8 *Ibid.*, pp. 336, 338, 379.

9 Davidson, *History of the Presbyterian Church in Kentucky*, p. 189.

10 Cf. Sweet, *The Rise of Methodism in the West*, pp. 13 ff.

11 Mode, *The Frontier Spirit in American Christianity*, pp. 132 ff.

12 Lee, *History of Methodism*, p. 107. Quoted in Buckley, *A History of Methodists in the United States*, p. 246.

13 Buckley, p. 246; Luccock and Hutchinson, *The Story of Methodism*, p. 247.

NOTES

[14] Bacon, *op. cit.*, pp. 200-201.

[15] Buckley, *op. cit.*, pp. 281 ff., 325 ff.; Luccock and Hutchinson, *op. cit.*, pp. 274 ff.

[16] Brunson, Alfred, *A Western Pioneer*, Vol. I, p. 43.

[17] Bacon, *op. cit.*, p. 148.

[18] Bacon, *op. cit.*, pp. 201 f.; Buckley, *op. cit.*, pp. 181, 198.

[19] Cf. Sweet, *op. cit.*, p. 35; Cleveland, *op. cit.*, p. 148.

[20] Cf. Sweet, *op. cit.*, Ch. II.

[21] Luccock and Hutchinson, *op. cit.*, p. 289; cf. pp. 289-292, 295-300.

[22] Cf. Tyler, *History of the Disciples of Christ*, *American Church History Series*, Vol. XII.

[23] Mode, *The Frontier Spirit in American Christianity*, pp. 106 ff.

[24] *U. S. Census, Religious Bodies, 1906, Bulletin 103*, p. 70.

[25] Weber, *Aufsätze zur Religionssoziologie*, Vol. I, pp. 255-256.

[26] Beard, *Rise of American Civilization*, Vol. I, p. 663.

[27] Channing, *History of the United States*, Vol. IV, pp. 430 ff.; Vol. V, pp. 121 ff.

[28] *Ibid.*, Vol. III, pp. 4-5.

[29] *Ibid.*, Vol. III, pp. 556 f., Vol. IV, p. 435.

[30] *Ibid.*, Vol. V, pp. 143-144.

[31] Cf. Newman, *History of the Baptist Churches*, p. 306.

[32] Newman, *op. cit.*, p. 305.

[33] Buckley, *A History of the Methodists in the United States*, p. 185.

[34] *Ibid.*, pp. 197, 244 f.

[35] Newman, *op. cit.*, p. 305.

[36] Buckley, *op. cit.*, p. 303.

[37] *Ibid.*, p. 335.

[38] *American Church History Series*, Vol. XI, pp. 9-10.

[39] *Ibid.*, p. 7.

[40] Cf. Buckley, *op. cit.*, Chs. XVI and XVII.

[41] Cf. Buckley, p. 465.

[42] Tiffany, *History of the Protestant Episcopal Church*, Ch. XVI, pp. 500-503.

[43] Jacobs, *History of the Lutheran Church in the United States*, p. 452.

[44] Cf. Jacobs, *op. cit.*, pp. 453, 505 ff.

[45] Cf. Thompson, *op. cit.*, p. 155; *American Church History Series*, Vol. XI, pp. 327-28.

[46] Thompson, *op. cit.*, p. 155.

[47] *American Church History Series*, XI, pp. 348 ff.; Thompson, p. 155.

[48] *American Church History Series*, XI, p. 351; Thompson, pp. 158-159.

CHAPTER EIGHT

[1] Cf. Huntington, *Civilization and Climate*, Ch. X.

[2] Weber, *Aufsätze zur Religionssoziologie*, Vol. I, pp. 207 ff.

NOTES

3 Cf. Thompson, *op. cit.*, pp. 63-67; Tiffany, *op. cit.*, Ch. XIII; *American Church History Series*, Vol. VIII, pp. 174 ff. (The Reformed Church in America); Jacobs, *op. cit.*, Chs. XIV and XVI; Bacon, *op. cit.*, pp. 210-211.

4 Thompson, *op. cit.*, pp. 160 f.; Tiffany, *op. cit.*, pp. 497 ff.

5 *U. S. Census, Religious Bodies, 1906*, Pt. II, pp. 591-592; *American Church History Series*, Vol. VIII, p. 212.

6 On the Lutheran churches see Jacobs, *op. cit., passim.* The statistics on the use of foreign languages in the U. S. Census reports are very instructive in this connection; cf. *Religious Bodies*, 1906, 1916, 1926.

7 Ross, *The Old World in the New*, pp. 75 f.

8 Jacobs, *op. cit.*, pp. 500-501; *U. S. Census, Religious Bodies, 1916*, Pt. II, *passim.*

9 *American Church History Series*, Vol. XI, pp. 172 ff.

10 Cf. Thompson, *op. cit.*, p. 47; *American Church History Series*, Vol. XI, pp. 168 f.

11 Thompson, *op. cit.*, pp. 76, 102 f., 104; cf. *American Church History Series*, XI, pp. 146, 156 f., 181, 155.

12 *American Church History Series*, Vol. XI, pp. 358-359.

13 Cf. Siegfried, *America Comes of Age.*

14 Cf. Fairchild, *Immigration*, Ch. XVI.

15 Cf. *Ecclesiastical Records of the State of New York*, Vol. V, pp. 3459-60, cf. Vol. VI, pp. 3853 ff.

16 Quoted in Jacobs, *History of the Lutheran Church*, p. 338.

17 *Ibid.*, p. 328.

18 Jacobs, *op. cit.*, pp. 330 f.

19 Dubbs, *History of the Reformed Church, German*, in *American Church History Series*, Vol. VIII, pp. 285 ff. Cf. Good, *History of the Reformed Church in the United States*, pp. 435 ff.

20 Dubbs, *op. cit.*, pp. 316-322, cf. pp. 343-345.

21 Jacobs, *op. cit.*, p. 320.

22 See above, pp. 144-145.

23 Bacon, *op. cit.*, p. 306.

24 *Ibid.*

25 *Ibid.*, pp. 304-309.

26 Tiffany, *History of the Protestant Episcopal Church*, p. 414, cf. Ch. XV.

27 Jacobs, *op. cit.*, Ch. XVII.

28 Cf. Jacobs, *op. cit.*, pp. 310-312.

29 *Ibid.*, p. 362.

30 Cf. Ferm, *The Crisis in American Lutheran Theology.*

CHAPTER NINE

1 U. S. Religious Census of 1926; *Negro Year Book*, 1925-26, pp. 262-63.

2 Cf. Dowd, *The Negro in American Life*, pp. 73 f.

NOTES

3 For a presentation of this bright side of the picture see Winston, G. T.: "The Relation of the White to the Negroes," in *Annals of the American Academy*, Vol. 18, pp. 105 ff.

4 Mode, *Source Book of American Church History*, pp. 549 ff.

5 Woodson, *History of the Negro Church*, pp. 6-7, 149-152.

6 Cf. Mode, *Source Book*, p. 552.

7 *Ibid.*, p. 197.

8 Cf. Woodson, *History of the Negro Church*, p. 10.

9 *Ibid.*, p. 17.

10 Quoted in Bragg, G. F., *History of the Afro-American Group of the Episcopal Church;* cf. pp. 33-38. Cf. also Woodson, *History of the Negro Church*, Ch. I.

11 Cf. Woodson, *op. cit.*, pp. 97, 152-158.

12 *Minutes*, p. 183, quoted in *Baird's Digest*, 1855, p. 828.

13 *Minutes of 1864*, p. 293. Quoted in *American Church History Series*, Vol. XI, p. 429.

14 *Minutes of 1865*, p. 370. Quoted in *American Church History Series*, Vol. XI, p. 378.

15 *American Church History Series*, Vol. XI, p. 379.

16 Thompson, *History of the Presbyterian Churches*, p. 193.

17 Cf. Bacon, *History of American Christianity*, pp. 154, 179, 246. Woodson, *History of the Negro Church*, pp. 23, 71.

18 *American Church History Series*, Vol. XI, p. 300.

19 Buckley, *A History of Methodists in the United States*, p. 294.

20 *Ibid.*, p. 597; cf. *American Church History Series*, Vol. XI, pp. 49, 69.

21 Cf. Woodson, *The Negro in Our History*, Ch. VIII, also p. 146.

22 Woodson, *History of the Negro Church*, pp. 53 ff.

23 Newman, *History of the Baptists*, p. 331.

24 *Ibid.*, p. 464.

25 Benedict, D., *A General History of the Baptist Denomination*, 1848, pp. 660, 661, 742, 756, 767, 771, note, *et passim*.

26 Cf. Woodson, *History of the Negro Church*, pp. 149 ff.; Bragg, *op. cit.*, pp. 36 f.

27 Mode, *Source Book*, pp. 549 f.

28 Woodson, *History of the Negro Church*, p. 61.

29 Cf. Mode, *op. cit.*, p. 551.

30 Cf. Woodson, *History of the Negro Church*, pp. 9 f.

31 Cf. Woodson, *The Negro in Our History*, pp. 90 ff., 146 f., 177 ff.

32 Mode, *op. cit.*, p. 551.

33 Woodson, *History of the Negro Church*, p. 27.

34 *Ibid.*, pp. 154 f. Cf. Woodson, *Negro Education*, Ch. II—"Religion With Letters," Ch. III—"Religion Without Letters."

35 Cf. Woodson, *Negro in Our History*, pp. 185 f.; *History of the Negro Church*, pp. 132 ff.

36 Cf. Bragg, *op. cit.*, pp. 38 f.

NOTES

37 Woodson, *History of the Negro Church, passim; Negro Year Book, 1925-26,* p. 256. The first Negro Baptist Church in America was organized at Silver Bluff, near Augusta, Georgia, in 1773.

38 Cf. Woodson, *History of the Negro Church,* Ch. IV; cf. Benedict, *op. cit.,* pp. 66, 662, 756.

39 Cf. Buckley, *op. cit.,* pp. 346 ff.; *Negro Year Book,* pp. 256 f.

40 Buckley, *op. cit.,* p. 579; *Am. Ch. Hist. Ser.,* Vol. XI, pp. 86, 91 f.

41 Woodson, *History of the Negro Church,* pp. 188-201; cf. the denominational histories in the *American Church History Series.*

42 Allen's account, reprinted in Bragg, *op. cit.,* pp. 47 f.

43 *Discipline* of the A.M.E. Zion Church.

44 Davenport, *Primitive Traits in Religious Revivals,* Ch. V— "The Religion of the American Negro"; Dowd, *The Negro in American Life,* pp. 178 f.

CHAPTER TEN

1 Cf. Keller and Stewart, *Protestant Europe;* Rowland, *Native Churches in Foreign Fields.*

INDEX

Abolition movement, 190

Accommodation, 136, 186, 201, 203-220

Activism in religion, 83 f., 96, 203-204

Adeney, W. F., 116 f., 289

African Methodist Episcopal Church, 239, 257

African Methodist Episcopal Zion Church, 239, 255-256, 257, 260 f.

Agriculture. See *Rural*

Albright, Jacob, 164

Allen, Richard, 255, 257, 260

American Christianity, its denominations, 106-108; social factors in, 135-136; its activism, 204 f., its form of organization, 207, 211; future development, 271-272. See also *Frontier Immigration, Race, Sectionalism*

Americanization, 200, 201, 212, 216, 220, 226

Anabaptists, 34 ff., 44, 46, 51

Anglican Church. See *Church of England*

Antinomians, 46

Arianism, 113

Armenian Christianity, 113

Arminianism, 103, 104, 144-145, 158, 176, 230

Asbury, Francis, 173, 174

Asceticism, 55, 91

Associate Presbytery, 218

Associate Reformed Church, 218

Athanasius, 113

Augsburg Confession, 127, 217, 232

Bacon, Leonard, 173 f., 230, 231, 290, 291, 292, 293, 294

Backus, Isaac, 168, 290, 291

Baptists, General, 40, 168

Baptists, in New England, 152; on the frontier, 166, 167 ff.; in Rhode Island, 167; their growth after Great Awakening, 168; in the Southwest, 169-170; their accommodation to new conditions, 170; early attitude toward slavery, 191-192; accommodation to slavery, 193-194; slavery schism, 194-195; changes in doctrine, 230; attitude toward Negroes, 246 f., 248, 250, 256, 258; schism of white and Negro groups, 236. See also *Anabaptists*

Barclay, R., 286, 287

Bax, Belfort, 38, 285

Baxter, Richard, 44, 286, 287

Beard, Charles, 164, 188-189, 290, 292

Benedict, D., 274, 294

Berens, L., 286, 287

"Birthright membership," 21

Bohemia, 119

Bonwetsch, N., 289

Bourgeoisie. See *Middle Classes*

Buckley, J. M., 291, 292, 294, 295

Burghers and Anti-Burghers, 218

Bragg, G. F., 294, 295

Brunson, Alfred, 175, 292

Brownists, 43 f.

Bryan, Wm. J., 184

Calvin, John, 41, 95 f., 98, 133, 286

Calvinism, 10 f., 16, 29, 41 f.; a middle-class movement, ch. iv; and capitalism, 79 ff.,

INDEX

Eastern national churches, 113

Eastern Orthodox Churches, 10, 113-117, 125

Eastern religions, 268-269

Economic interpretation of religious history, 26, 27

Eddy, Mary Baker, 90

Edwards, Jonathan, 104

Elliott, Bishop Stephen, 242

Emigration. See *Immigration*

Episcopalianism, 15. See also *Church of England, Protestant Episcopal Church*

Ethical synthesis, 22, 266-268

Ethnic factors in denominationalism, 107, 108-109

Evangelical Synod of North America, 215-216

Evangelical Church, 163

Evangelical party, 62, 65, 69

Evangelistic societies, 75-76

Family ethics, 86 f.

Ferm, V., 293

Feudalism, 120

Federalism, 153, 175

Fifth Monarchy Men, 48, 49

Fisher, G. P., 57, 287, 289

Fox, George, 47, 48, 50, 52, 283

Franciscan movement, 283

Free-Will Baptists, 168

French nationalism and Roman Catholicism, 118 f.

Friends. See *Quakers*

Frontier, and denominationalism, 137, 140 ff.; significance for American culture, 137-138; conflict with established society, 138-140; religious psychology, 140-145; sectarian organization, 143; ethics, 143; influence on denominations, 145-146; and the Great Awakening, 149-151; in New England, 148-152; in the Southwest, 157-161; and the German churches, 162-163; as a source of sectarianism, 163-164; and Methodist, Baptist and Disciples churches, 165-187; its inter-denominationalism, 179; its transition to agricultural economy, 181; attitude toward Negro, 244 ff.

Fundamentalism, 184, 186

Geneva, 99, 101

German churches in America, 162-163, 202, 204, 205 ff., 211 ff., 214-216, 217, 226-229, 231-234

German Evangelical Synod of North America, 215 f.

German immigrants, 222, 226-228

German nationalism and Roman Catholicism, 117 f.

German Reformed Church, 226, 227-229, 233

Gooch, G. P., 286, 287

Good, James I., 293

Great Awakening, 149, 167, 168, 230

Greek influence on theology, 11 f., 16

Greek Orthodox Church, 113, 114. See also *Eastern Orthodox Churches*

Greek patriotism and religion, 113

Gregory VII, 117 f.

Grotius, Hugo, 103

Guignebert, C., 112 f., 289

"Half-Way Covenant," 20, 148, 151

Hall, T. C., 287

Harnack, Adolf, 285, 289

Harrison, Thomas, 47, 48, 49

Henson, Canon, 286

Hoffmann, Melchior, 34

Hobart, Bishop, 230-231

Holy Roman Empire, 117 f., 122

Humanism, 99, 101 f., 121

Huntingdon, Countess of, 61

Huntington, Ellsworth, 292

Hus, John, 119

INDEX

sonianism, 175; distribution of
its membership, 176; in the
Southwest, 176 ff.; and the
slavery schisms, 191-195; and
the Negro, 245-246, 248, 250,
251, 258

Methodist Episcopal Church,
South, 191-195, 236, 245,
257 f.

Methodist Protestant Church,
174

Middle Classes, 34, ch. iv; religious psychology of, 80-85;
ethics of, 85 f.; polity of middle-class churches, 88; and
Calvinism, 95 ff.; and rationalism, 101 ff.

Millenarians in England, 46, 49

Millenarianism, 31, 74, 76, 82

Milton, John, 43, 45

Missionary churches, 271-272,
273

Mode, P. G., 290, 291, 294

Modernism, 184, 186

Mormonism, 160

Mueller, Karl, 289

Muenzer, Thomas, 34

Muhlenberg, H. M., 232

Nationalism, ethnic factors in,
108-110; its cultural aspects,
110 f.; and denominationalism,
9, 10, 22 ff., 265, 271, 273, 280;
and early heresies, 113; and
Eastern Orthodox Churches,
113-116; and Roman Catholic
Church, 117-122; and the
Reformation, 121 ff.; and humanism, 121; and economic
development of Europe, 121

National Baptist Convention,
239, 258

National churches, their characteristics, 124-132; their
modern growth, 271-272

Negroes, in white denominations
before Civil War, 240-247;
opposition to their evangelization, 248-251; regulation of
their religious meetings, 252;
their segregation in mixed
churches, 254-255; founding
of their independent churches,
255-263; their religious psychology, 262. See also *Slavery, Race*

New England, 99, 147

Newman, A. H., 193, 247, 290,
291, 292, 294

New Thought, 104

Nietzsche, F., 77

Non-resistance, 39, 52 f., 280

Northern and Southern
churches, 187-199

O'Kelley, James, 174

Otterbein, Philip, 164

Paxson, F. N., 139, 290

Peasants' War, 34 ff.

Pease, T. C., 286, 287

Pharisees and Sadducees, 13

Pilgrims, 43 f.

Political factors in denominationalism, 111 ff., 191, 195-
198. See also *State-churches*

Polity, and the New Testament,
14 f.; social sources of, 15; of
churches of the poor, 19; of
middle-class churches, 88; of
immigrant churches, 207 f.;
of frontier churches, 143. See
also *State-churches, Separation of church and state*

Predestination, 84-85, 100, 144 f.
See also *Arminianism*

Poor, the, 77, 141, 142; their
religious neglect, 28; as orig-
inators of religious movements, 29 ff.; their psychology
and ethics, 30-31; and early
Christianity, 32; and Roman
Catholicism, 33; and the
Reformation, 34-38; and the
Anabaptist movement, 38-39;
in 17th century England, 39-
53; and Methodism, 54-72;
in modern times, 72-76

Protestantism, 34 ff., 92, 109.
See also *Reformation*

INDEX

INDEX

LIVING AGE BOOKS

Published by MERIDIAN BOOKS, INC.
17 Union Square West, New York 3, N. Y.

LIVING AGE BOOKS, a new series of inexpensive editions published by MERIDIAN BOOKS, INC., will contain works of proven merit on history, art, literature, theology, and Biblical studies, as they illuminate the development of Christian tradition in the West. Ask your bookseller for these sewn-bound volumes. (Titles listed here are not necessarily available in the British Empire.)